100

FAST & FOOLPROOF

FRESHWATER

FISH RECIPES

100

FAST & FOOLPROOF

FRESHWATER

FISH RECIPES

HENRY SINKUS

WILLOW CREEK PRESS®

Published by Willow Creek Press
P.O. Box 147, Minocqua, Wisconsin 54548

For information on other Willow Creek Press titles,
call 1-800-850-9453

Printed in The United States of America

TABLE OF CONTENTS

INTRODUCTION

It was not all that long ago that the average person's diet was determined by one's ability to harvest wild foods. Fishing provided a significant portion of the table fare. As time went by, fishing was no longer considered a necessity but, rather, a sport, a choice that provides more than food for the table, but revitalization of the spirit, a connection with traditions and techniques taught by our parents and grandparents, a choice that nourishes the body and satisfies the soul.

Freshwater fish is a very healthy alternative to meat. Fish is naturally high in protein, vitamins and minerals and low in calories and cholesterol.

The recipes in this book are, for the most part, quick and easy, without complicated procedures and time-consuming steps. Thank you for inviting me into your kitchen. I have enjoyed writing this book and I sincerely hope you find it to be informative, the recipes to be instructive and your results delicious.

—Henry Sinkus

All of the fish used in this book's recipes can be replaced with other fish. Fish generally falls into two categories, oily fish and lean fish. When substituting fish in a recipe, best results can be achieved by using a fish from the same category. For example, if your recipe calls for Walleye, you can use Pan Fish, Northern Pike or Bass instead. The chart below is a brief list of the most common freshwater fish by type:

LEAN FISHES

BASS, NORHTERN PIKE, WALLEYE, PERCH, SAUGER,
BLUEGILL, CRAPPIE, SUNFISH, ROCK BASS,
CATFISH, FLATHEAD, CHANNELCAT,
SUCKERS, STURGEON

OILY FISHES

SALMON, TROUT, HERRING, BLUE FISH

APPETIZERS & STARTERS

WHITEFISH AND GUACAMOLE DIP

SERVES 4-6

INGREDIENTS
- 1 cup cooked whitefish, flaked
- 1 ripe avocado, peeled, seeded and mashed
- 1 tablespoon lemon juice
- onion salt to taste
- garlic powder to taste
- fresh ground pepper to taste
- ⅓ cup medium salsa

TO KEEP THE DIP FROM TURNING BROWN, PLACE THE AVOCADO SEED IN THE CENTER OF THE BOWL.

DIRECTIONS
Sprinkle mashed avocado with lemon juice. Mix thoroughly with the onion salt, garlic powder, pepper and salsa. Fold in the flaked whitefish. Serve at once. Makes 1½ to 2 cups.

BUFFET SALMON

SERVES 14-20

INGREDIENTS
- 1 whole head-on dressed salmon, 4–6 pounds
- 4 tablespoons olive oil
- salt and pepper
- juice of 2 lemons
- 1 bunch fresh parsley

DIRECTIONS
Rinse the salmon inside and out and dry it well. Cut the fish in half at a slight diagonal. Sprinkle with lemon juice and season, inside and out, with salt and pepper. Stuff with parsley.

Place the salmon halves on oiled sheets of heavy aluminum foil, large enough to make sealed pouches. Close and seal the pouches. Place in shallow baking pans.

Bake in a 350 degree oven for 10–12 minutes for each inch of thickness. Check for doneness after ⅔ of the cooking time has passed. The internal temperature should be 165 degrees. (Check temperature by piercing the foil at the thickest part of the fish. If additional time is required, seal the foil with a piece of foil dipped in egg wash.)

Remove the fish packets from the oven and carefully poke a hole in the foil to allow the steam to escape. Refrigerate for several hours or overnight before serving.

Unwrap and plate the salmon, matching the cut halves. Remove the parsley and peel off the skin starting at the tail. Garnish with dill fronds and lemon wedges.

IF YOU DON'T HAVE A SERVING PLATTER LARGE ENOUGH TO ACCOMMODATE THE WHOLE SALMON, USE A 12"X24" MELAMINE-COVERED SHELF BOARD, AVAILABLE AT MOST HARDWARE STORES OR LUMBAR YARDS. THIS MAKES AN INEXPENSIVE SERVING PLATTER THAT IS EASILY CLEANED AND CAN BE USED MANY TIMES.

SMOKED WHITEFISH AND CREAM CHEESE SPREAD

SERVES 4-6

INGREDIENTS

- ½ pound boneless, skinless smoked whitefish, cut into chunks
- 3 tablespoons onion, chopped
- 1 tablespoon capers
- 8 ounces cream cheese, softened
- few drops hot sauce, to taste

DIRECTIONS

In a food processor fitted with a stainless blade, pulse chop the whitefish, onion and capers until finely minced. Add the cream cheese and process until smooth. Adjust flavor with the hot sauce. Transfer to a serving bowl, cover with plastic wrap and refrigerate at least one hour before serving. Makes about 2 cups.

FOR A SMOOTHER, LESS GRAINY TEXTURE,
ADD 2 TABLESPOONS HEAVY CREAM
DURING PROCESSING.

LOMI LOMI SALMON
(HAWAIIAN LUAU SALMON)

INGREDIENTS

- 2 cups salt-cured or gravlax salmon, skin removed and cut into ½-inch dice
- 3 Roma tomatoes, seeded and cut into ½-inch dice
- 1 medium sweet onion, diced
- 2 green onions, thinly sliced

DIRECTIONS

Mix all ingredients and serve in a bowl placed in a larger bowl of crushed ice.

FOR A MORE FORMAL PRESENTATION, REDUCE THE DICE
SIZE TO 1/4-INCH. CUT THE TOPS FROM CHERRY TOMATOES,
REMOVE THE PULP AND DRY THE TOMATO SHELLS.
FILL THE TOMATOES WITH THE SALMON MIXTURE.

WHITEFISH CEVICHE

SERVES 4

INGREDIENTS

- 1 pound boneless, skinless whitefish fillets, cut into ¼-inch cubes
- juice of 6 limes
- 4 Roma tomatoes, peeled, seeded and cut into ¼-inch dice
- 1 4-ounce can diced green chilies
- ⅓ cup sweet onion, minced
- ¼ cup olive oil
- 1 teaspoon salt
- cayenne pepper or tabasco to taste
- shredded lettuce

THIS MAKES A WONDERFUL HORS D'OEUVRES SERVED WITH FANCY CRACKERS OR COCKTAIL RYE BREAD.

DIRECTIONS

Place whitefish in a large sealable plastic bag. Place bag in a large bowl. Pour in the lime juice, seal the bag and refrigerate at least 4 hours. Turn the bag several times.

Drain the fish, discarding the lime juice, and combine with the tomatoes, chilies, onion, olive oil and salt. Season to taste with the cayenne or tabasco. Serve on shredded lettuce.

SMOKED SALMON SPREAD

INGREDIENTS

* 1 pound boneless, skinless smoked salmon
* 1 small onion, minced
* 1 tablespoon capers
* ¼ pound unsalted butter, softened
* 3 drops hot sauce

DIRECTIONS

In a food processor fitted with a stainless blade, pulse chop the salmon, onion and capers until finely minced. Add the butter and hot sauce. Process until smooth. Transfer to a serving bowl, cover and refrigerate for at least 2 hours.

Before serving, bring to room temperature. Serve with crackers or toast rounds. Makes about 3 cups.

REPLACE THE BUTTER WITH 8 OUNCES OF
SOFTENED CREAM CHEESE FOR A COMPLETELY
DIFFERENT FLAVOR AND TEXTURE.

WALLEYE MOUSSE

SERVES 6-8

INGREDIENTS

- ½ pound cooked walleye
- ¼ cup heavy cream
- 2 tablespoons chives
- 2 tablespoons red onion, minced
- 2 tablespoon fresh lemon juice
- salt and pepper

A QUICK AND EASY APPETIZER. TO COOK THE WALLEYE, USE YOUR MICROWAVE.

DIRECTIONS

In a food processor fitted with a stainless blade, pulse chop the fish, chives, onion and lemon juice. With the processor running, slowly pour in the cream, and process until the mixture thickens, 1–2 minutes. Season with salt and pepper to taste.

Place the mousse in a serving dish. Cover and refrigerate at least 2 hours. Serve with whole wheat crackers or toast rounds.

SALT-CURED SALMON (GRAVLAX)

INGREDIENTS
- 2 salmon fillets, 2–2½ pounds each, skin on
- 1 cup kosher salt
- ½ cup light brown granulated sugar
- 1½ tablespoons dried dill weed
- 3 tablespoons coarsely ground black pepper

GRAVLAX CAN BE WRAPPED AND FROZEN. IF VACUUM SEALED, YOU WILL HAVE A MORE SATISFACTORY FROZEN PRODUCT.

DIRECTIONS
Mix the salt, sugar, dill and pepper together.

Place one salmon fillet skin side down, in a glass dish or stainless steel pan—do not use aluminum! Evenly coat the fillet with ½ of the salt mixture. Turn the fillet skin side up. Place the 2nd fillet skin side down on top of the first fillet, head over tail, to achieve uniform thickness. Coat the second fillet with the remaining salt mixture.

Cover with plastic wrap, then a second dish or pan to which you will add about 4 pounds of weight. Cover with foil and refrigerate for 24 hours.

Take out of refrigerator and remove the foil, weighted pan and plastic wrap. Drain the liquid and turn the fillets over as one unit. Cover with plastic wrap, replace the weighted pan and cover with foil. Repeat the draining and turning steps 2 more times, 24 hours apart.

On the 4th day, scrape the salt mixture from the fillets. Cover with plastic wrap and wrap in foil. Gravlax can be kept in the refrigerator for a maximum of 2 weeks.

To carve, place a fillet skin side down on a cutting board. Using a very sharp fillet or thin carving knife held at a slight angle, slice thin strips turning the knife to free the strips from the skin. Sprinkle the slices with lime juice and serve with crackers.

GRILLED SMELT

SERVES 4

INGREDIENTS
- **12 large smelt, dressed and head removed**
- **12 bacon strips**
- **12 lemon wedges**
- **salt and pepper to taste**

DIRECTIONS
Season the smelt inside and out with salt and pepper. Spiral wrap a strip of bacon around each smelt, securing the ends with a round toothpick.

Spray the grill with non-stick cooking spray. Heat the grill to high and reduce heat to medium. Grill the smelt 10 minutes on each side or until the bacon is just crisp

DON'T HAVE A GRILL? PRECOOK THE BACON AND BAKE
THE SMELT AT 350 DEGREES FOR 20 MINUTES OR
UNTIL BACON IS DONE TO YOUR LIKING.

SMOKED SALMON DIP

SERVES 8-10

INGREDIENTS
- 8 ounces boneless, skinless smoked salmon
- 1 8-ounce package cream cheese at room temperature
- 2 tablespoons minced onion
- 1 teaspoon horseradish
- ½ teaspoon dijon mustard

DIRECTIONS
Blend all ingredients in a food processor until smooth. Transfer to a serving dish and chill several hours before serving.

FOR A FANCIER PRESENTATION, REFRIGERATE THE DIP FOR 1 HOUR.
FORM INTO A BALL OR LOG AND ROLL IN FINELY CHOPPED NUTS.
WRAP IN PLASTIC WRAP AND REFRIGERATE UNTIL FIRM.

A DATE WITH THE BAIT

This is an adaptation of a dish served on the streets of many Oriental cities.

INGREDIENTS
- 2½ pounds medium minnows
- 1 cup flour
- ½ teaspoon Cajun seasoning
- ½ teaspoon ground ginger
- pinch of salt
- vegetable oil

DIRECTIONS
In a large bowl, mix together the flour, Cajun seasoning and ginger. Coat the fish and shake off any excess flour mixture. Heat the oil to 375 degrees in a large pan or deep skillet. Fry the fish for 3 minutes or until golden and crisp. Drain well on a paper towel. Serve hot with lemon or lime wedges.

A SAUCE OF 1 CUP TERIYAKI AND 1/4 TEASPOON HOT SAUCE

IS A WONDERFUL ACCOMPANIMENT. IF YOU PREFER,

USE SMALL DRESSED SMELT INSTEAD OF MINNOWS.

ITALIAN STYLE BLUEGILL APPETIZERS

MAKES 30 APPETIZERS

INGREDIENTS

- ½ pound boneless, skinless bluegill fillets, cooked and flaked
- 1 loaf french bread (baguette), sliced diagonally into 30 pieces
- 4 tablespoons butter, softened
- 1 roasted red pepper, cut in fine strips
- 1 roasted yellow pepper, cut in fine strips
- 1 tablespoon olive oil
- 2 garlic cloves, crushed and minced
- ½ small onion, minced
- 2 tablespoons capers
- ⅓ cup sliced black olives
- 2 tablespoons pesto sauce
- 2 tablespoons lemon juice
- salt and freshly ground black pepper to taste
- chopped fresh parsley

USE COMMERCIALLY PREPARED PESTO AND STORE ANY UNUSED PORTION AS SEASONING IN YOUR NEXT ITALIAN DISH.

DIRECTIONS

Lightly butter the baguette slices. Place them, butter side up, on a baking sheet and bake in the center of a 325 degree oven for 10–12 minutes or until lightly browned.

In a heavy skillet, heat the oil and sauté the onion and garlic until soft. Remove from heat and add the peppers, capers, olives, pesto and lemon juice. Mix in the fish and season to taste with salt and pepper.

Spread about 2 teaspoons of the fish mixture on each baguette slice. Garnish with chopped fresh parsley.

HAWAIIAN STYLE BASS CEVICHE

SERVES 4-6

INGREDIENTS
- **12 ounces boneless, skinless bass fillets, cut into ½-inch cubes**
- **1 cup freshly squeezed lime juice**
- **½ cup freshly squeezed orange juice**
- **2 tablespoons olive oil**
- **3 tablespoons freshly chopped cilantro**
- **2 Hawaiian chili peppers, chopped**
- **½ cup green onion, cut into ¼-inch lengths**
- **Hawaiian salt to taste**
- **½ large ripe papaya, peeled, seeded and diced**
- **½ large ripe avocado, peeled, seeded and diced**
- **lime wedges**
- **lettuce leaves**

DIRECTIONS
Marinate the bass in the lime juice and refrigerate for 45 minutes. Drain off excess lime juice and discard. In a small bowl, add the orange juice, olive oil, cilantro, chili peppers, green onion and Hawaiian salt to the marinated bass fillets. Mix well and chill until ice-cold. Just before serving, add the papaya and avocado and gently mix. Present on a serving plate lined with lettuce and garnished with lime wedges.

REMOVE THE SKIN FROM FISH FILLETS WHILE THEY ARE FROZEN. LOOSEN AN EDGE OF SKIN AT THE TAIL UNDER SLOWLY RUNNING WATER. GRASP THE LOOSENED SKIN WITH PLIERS AND PULL THE SKIN AWAY FROM THE TAIL AND OFF THE FILLET. HOW EASY IS THAT?

SALMON CEVICHE

INGREDIENTS

- 1 pound boneless, skinless salmon fillets, thinly sliced
- 1 teaspoon brown sugar
- 2½ tablespoons sea salt
- ½ teaspoon chili paste
- ¼ cup freshly squeezed lime juice
- ¼ teaspoon pepper
- ¼ teaspoon cumin
- ¼ cup olive oil
- 1 clove garlic, minced
- ¼ cup red onion, minced
- 2 tablespoons cilantro, minced
- 1 avocado, sliced
- 1 tomato, diced
- 2 cups shredded lettuce

CEVICHE IS AN ACQUIRED TASTE, BUT IS A VERY HEALTHY SNACK OR MEAL.

DIRECTIONS

In a large glass or plastic bowl, mix the lime juice, brown sugar, sea salt and chili paste. Stir in the pepper, cumin, olive oil, garlic, onion, tomato and cilantro. Gently mix in the salmon. Cover and refrigerate for at least 4 hours.

To serve, drain and discard the excess liquid from the salmon. Let rest at room temperature for 15 minutes. Place the lettuce in the center of a large serving platter with the ceviche arranged on top.

SALADS

SALMON MACARONI SALAD

SERVES 6

INGREDIENTS
- 3 cups cooked macaroni or other small pasta shape
- 1 pound poached salmon fillet
- 3 boiled eggs, chopped
- 2 stalks celery, chopped
- 1 10-ounce package frozen baby peas
- 1 medium onion, chopped
- 1 green pepper, seeded and chopped
- 3 green onions, sliced and chopped

DRESSING
- ⅓ cup creamy Italian dressing
- 1 cup mayonnaise
- ½ cup sour cream
- ½ teaspoon granulated garlic
- ½ teaspoon salt
- ⅛ teaspoon white pepper

DIRECTIONS
In a small bowl, mix together the dressing ingredients and refrigerate for 1 hour.

In a large bowl, mix together the salad ingredients. Fold in the dressing.

FOR A TROPICAL FLAVOR, SERVE ON PINEAPPLE SLICES. THIS SALAD IS HEARTY ENOUGH TO BE SERVED AS A COLD ENTRÉE ON A WARM SUMMER DAY.

CRAYFISH AND RICE MOUSSE

SERVES 6

INGREDIENTS

- ¾ pound crayfish tails, cooked, shelled and chopped
- ¼ teaspoon Old Bay seasoning
- 1 package unflavored gelatin
- 6 tablespoons mayonnaise
- 2 teaspoons lemon juice
- ½ cup heavy cream
- ¼ cup green onion, minced
- ½ cup whole-kernel corn, cooked and drained
- 1½ cups rice, cooked and chilled
- lettuce leaves

DIRECTIONS

Prepare gelatin according to package directions. Stir in the mayonnaise, seasoning and lemon juice. Refrigerate until gelatin begins to set. Beat the mixture until light and fluffy. Whip the cream until stiff and fold into the gelatin mixture.

Add the green onion, corn, rice and crayfish and blend carefully. Pour the mixture into a lightly oiled mold and chill until set. Unmold and serve on lettuce leaves

USE A PAN SPRAY TO OIL YOUR MOLD.

THE GELATIN WILL RELEASE MUCH EASIER.

WHITEFISH LOUIS

INGREDIENTS

- 3 cups cooked whitefish, flaked
- 2 cups sliced iceberg lettuce
- 2 cups sliced romaine lettuce
- 2 Roma tomatoes, cut into wedges
- 2 hard boiled eggs, sliced
- ¼ cup sliced black olives

DRESSING

- ¾ cup mayonnaise
- 4 tablespoons ketchup
- ⅓ cup sour cream
- 2 tablespoons heavy cream
- 2 tablespoons green onion, sliced
- 1 tablespoon sweet pickle relish
- 1 teaspoon lemon juice
- 1 teaspoon worcestershire sauce

QUICK, HEALTHY AND DELICIOUS. THE PERFECT MEAL FOR WARM SUMMER NIGHTS.

DIRECTIONS

In a medium bowl, combine all dressing ingredients and mix well. Cover and refrigerate for at least 1 hour.

Mix lettuce and arrange on a service plate. Mound fish in the center. Arrange tomato wedges, egg slices and olives around the fish. Ladle half the dressing over the fish. Serve remaining dressing on the side.

PERCH SALAD

INGREDIENTS

- 2 pounds boneless, skinless perch fillets, poached
- 1 cup mayonnaise
- ½ cup red onion, minced
- ½ cup celery, minced
- ⅓ cup green pepper, seeded and diced
- ⅓ cup red pepper, seeded and diced
- ⅓ cup radish, diced
- 2 tablespoons chives, minced
- 2 hard-boiled eggs, chopped
- juice and zest of 1 lemon
- salt and pepper to taste
- lettuce leaves

DIRECTIONS

Cut the poached perch fillets into ½-inch cubes. In a large bowl, mix the mayonnaise with the lemon juice and salt and pepper. Mix in the onion, celery, green pepper, red pepper, radish and chives and gently fold in the fish.

Serve on the lettuce leaves and garnish with chopped egg and lemon zest.

SERVE AS A LIGHT LUNCH AND USE
LEFTOVERS FOR SNACK SANDWICHES.

MOLDED LAKE TROUT SALAD

INGREDIENTS

- 1½ cups lake trout, cooked and flaked
- 1 15-ounce can pineapple chunks, drained, saving ¼ cup of the liquid
- ½ cup celery, diced
- 1 red apple, unpeeled, cored and diced
- ¼ cup black olives, chopped
- 1 envelope unflavored gelatin
- 1 tablespoon cold water
- ¾ cup boiling water
- 1 tablespoon lemon juice
- 1 cup mayonnaise
- salt to taste
- chopped lettuce

DIRECTIONS

Combine fish, pineapple, celery, apple and olives in a mixing bowl. In a separate bowl, mix the gelatin with 1 tablespoon cold water. Add the boiling water and stir until gelatin is dissolved. Add the liquid from the pineapple and the lemon juice.

Combine the gelatin mixture with the mayonnaise and stir into the fish mixture. Add salt to taste. Pour into a lightly-oiled mold and refrigerate for at least 6 hours Unmold on a bed of chopped lettuce.

FOR A MORE ROBUST FLAVOR, SUBSTITUTE WHITE
WINE FOR THE WATER IN THE GELATIN. THE WINE
CAN BE EASILY HEATED IN THE MICROWAVE.

SALMON MOUSSE WITH CAPERS

SERVES 4-6

INGREDIENTS

- ½ pound cooked salmon, cut into cubes
- ¼ cup heavy cream
- 2 tablespoons chives, chopped
- 2 tablespoons sweet onion, minced
- 2 tablespoons lime juice
- 3 tablespoons capers, drained
- salt and pepper
- shredded lettuce

IF YOU DON'T HAVE CAPERS,
TRY USING GREEN OLIVES.

DIRECTIONS

In a food processor fitted with a stainless steel blade, pulse chop the salmon, chives, onion, lime juice and capers. With the processor running slowly add the cream and process until thickened, 1–2 minutes. Season with salt and pepper to taste.

Place the mousse in a serving dish. Cover and refrigerate 2–3 hours before serving. Divide into equal servings and serve over shredded lettuce.

SMOKED LAKE TROUT SALAD

SERVES 4

INGREDIENTS

* 1½ pounds smoked lake trout, skin and bones removed, flaked
* 2 packages mixed field greens
* 12 grape tomatoes, cut in half
* 1 medium zucchini squash, peeled and thinly sliced

FOR A LOWER CALORIE DRESSING, SUBSTITUTE LOW FAT YOGURT FOR THE SOUR CREAM.

DRESSING

* ⅛ teaspoon dry mustard
* 2 teaspoons dijon mustard
* 1½ tablespoons white wine vinegar
* 3 tablespoons olive oil
* ⅔ cup sour cream
* ½ teaspoon sugar

DIRECTIONS

In a small bowl, combine dry and dijon mustard. Whisk in remaining dressing ingredients. Cover and refrigerate 1 hour.

Divide the spring mix among 4 individual salad plates. Arrange equal portions of tomato and zucchini on each plate. Top with 1 ounce of the dressing and equal portions of the flaked smoked trout. Serve immediately with extra dressing on the side.

CRAYFISH WALDORF SALAD

SERVES 4

INGREDIENTS
- ½ cup dried cranberries
- ½ cup apple juice
- 2 tablespoons cream sherry
- 1 tablespoon lemon juice
- 1 large red apple, unpeeled, cored and cut into small pieces
- 2 cups crayfish tails, cooked, peeled and chopped
- 1 cup celery, chopped
- ⅓ cup walnut pieces
- ½ cup mayonnaise
- lettuce leaves

DIRECTIONS
Soak dried cranberries overnight in the apple juice and sherry. Sprinkle lemon juice over the diced apple, mixing well to avoid browning. Combine the crayfish, apples, celery, walnuts and cranberries. Mix in the mayonnaise and serve over lettuce leaves.

FOR ADDITIONAL COLOR AND FLAVOR, TRY ADDING
MANDARIN ORANGES. IF YOU ARE USING CANNED
ORANGES, DRAIN THEM THOROUGHLY.

BLUEGILL AND VEGETABLE SALAD

SERVES 6

INGREDIENTS

- 1½ cups cooked bluegill fillets, cut into ½-inch pieces
- 1 3-ounce package lemon-flavored gelatin
- salt to taste
- 1 cup boiling water
- 1 tablespoon lemon juice
- 1 tablespoon dry sherry
- ¾ cup ice-cold chicken stock
- ¼ cup carrots, grated
- ¼ cup green pepper, chopped
- ½ cup celery, minced
- lettuce leaves

DIRECTIONS

In a medium bowl, mix together the gelatin and salt. Add the boiling water and stir until the gelatin is dissolved. Stir in the lemon juice, sherry and stock. Let this mixture cool.

Add the carrot, pepper, celery and fish. Pour into a lightly-oiled shallow rectangular dish and refrigerate 4 hours or until set. Cut into portions and place on lettuce leaves.

FOR AN EASY DRESSING, MIX 1/2 CUP
MAYONNAISE WITH 1 TEASPOON OLD BAY
SEASONING AND 1/4 CUP SOUR CREAM.

CATFISH, CRAYFISH, NUT AND FRUIT MOLD

INGREDIENTS
- ½ pound crayfish tails, cooked, peeled and chopped
- ½ pound cooked catfish, cut into 1-inch pieces
- 1 tablespoon grapefruit juice
- 2 tablespoons orange juice
- 1 small bottle clam juice
- 1 3-ounce package lime-flavored gelatin
- ¾ cup boiling water
- ½ cup seedless grapes, chilled
- ½ cup peeled grapefruit sections, chilled
- ½ cup peeled orange sections, chilled
- ½ cup toasted slivered almonds
- ¼ cup mayonnaise
- 1 3-ounce package cream cheese, softened
- shredded lettuce

DIRECTIONS
Pour the clam juice, grapefruit juice and orange juice into a medium bowl. Place in the freezer to get ice-cold. Dissolve gelatin in boiling water and add the ice-cold juice mixture, stirring well. Let stand until it begins to set. Mix catfish, crayfish, fruit and nuts together. Stir into gelatin. Using an electric mixer, blend the mayonnaise and cream cheese until smooth and stir into the gelatin mixture. Pour into a 5-cup mold. Chill for 2–24 hours, unmold onto a bed of lettuce and serve.

ANY CITRUS-FLAVORED GELATIN WILL WORK WITH THIS
RECIPE. STAY AWAY FROM FRUIT-FLAVORED GELATIN.

SOUPS, STEWS & CHOWDERS

CATFISH GUMBO

SERVES 6

INGREDIENTS

- 1 pound boneless, skinless catfish fillets, cut into 1-inch pieces
- ½ cup celery, chopped
- ½ cup green pepper, chopped
- ½ cup onion, chopped
- ¼ cup vegetable oil
- 2 beef bouillon cubes
- 2 cups boiling water
- 1 15-ounce can stewed tomatoes
- 1 10-ounce package frozen okra, thawed and sliced
- 2 teaspoons salt
- ¾ teaspoon pepper
- ¼ teaspoon dried thyme
- dash of Tabasco sauce
- 1½ cups cooked rice

ADD DICED, COOKED CHORIZO SAUSAGE TO THE RICE FOR ADDED CAJUN FLAVOR.

DIRECTIONS

In a large saucepan, cook celery, green pepper, onion and garlic in oil until tender. Dissolve bouillon cubes in the boiling water and add to the saucepan along with the tomatoes, okra and seasonings. Cover and simmer 20 minutes.

Place the fish on the vegetables. Cover and simmer for an additional 15 minutes or until the fish flakes.

Place ¼ cup rice in each of 6 bowls and top with the gumbo.

CREAM OF SALMON SOUP

INGREDIENTS

- 1½ cups cooked salmon, flaked
- 4 cups fish stock or 1 cup of water and 3 cups chicken stock
- 2 cans condensed cream of mushroom soup
- ½ cup heavy cream
- 1 small package frozen mixed vegetables
- minced parsley

DIRECTIONS

Combine fish stock and condensed soup. Heat and stir constantly until smooth. Add the salmon and frozen vegetables. Simmer for 5 minutes, stirring occasionally, or until vegetables are hot. Remove from heat and stir in cream. Garnish with parsley.

FOR A COMPLETELY DIFFERENT
FLAVOR, USE CREAM OF CELERY
OR CREAM OF TOMATO SOUP.

FISH SOUP WITH ORZO PASTA

SERVES 4

INGREDIENTS
- 1 pound boneless, skinless fish fillets
  (perch, walleye, trout, bass—your choice), cut into 1-inch cubes
- 3 tablespoons olive oil
- 2 garlic cloves, chopped
- 1 onion, chopped
- 1 cup celery, diced
- 1 cup fennel bulb, sliced y-inch thick
- ½ cup dry white wine
- 6 cups fish stock
- 2 15-ounce cans stewed tomatoes, chopped
- ⅔ cup orzo pasta
- salt and pepper to taste
- ¼ cup fennel sprigs, chopped

DIRECTIONS
In a large saucepan, heat the oil and brown the garlic, onion, celery and fennel bulb. Add the wine and the stock and bring to a boil. Add the pasta and tomatoes and continue cooking until the pasta is tender. Season with salt and pepper. Add the fish and continue cooking for 3–5 minutes.

Check the seasoning, adjust as necessary and add the fennel sprigs just before serving.

IF FISH STOCK IS NOT AVAILABLE, USE 5 CUPS
LOW SODIUM CHICKEN STOCK AND 2 SMALL
BOTTLES OF CLAM JUICE AS A SUBSTITUTE.

SMOKED SALMON AND POTATO BISQUE

SERVES 6-8

INGREDIENTS

- 1 pound boneless, skinless smoked salmon, flaked
- 1 large onion, peeled, sliced and chopped
- 1 clove garlic, minced
- 1 stick butter, softened
- 3 medium potatoes, sliced and diced
- 4 cups chicken stock
- 4 cups heavy cream
- salt and pepper
- sliced green onion

DIRECTIONS

In a large dutch oven, melt the butter and sauté the onion until tender. Add the garlic, potatoes and chicken stock. Cook over medium heat until the potatoes are tender. Strain and save the stock.

Place the potato mixture and the salmon in a food processor. Pulse chop, adding 1 cup cream, and purée. Return the stock, puréed mixture and remaining cream to the dutch oven. Mix well and adjust seasoning to taste with salt and pepper. Reheat over low heat. Garnish with sliced green onion.

YOU CAN USE THIS RECIPE WITH JUST ABOUT ANY TYPE OF FRESHWATER FISH. IF YOU USE NON-SMOKED FISH, ADD A TOUCH OF NUTMEG FOR A NORTHWOODS FLAVOR.

HOMESTYLE FISH CHOWDER

SERVES 6-8

INGREDIENTS
- 1 pound pan fish fillets, cut into bite-size pieces
- 1 stick butter, softened
- 2 large onions, peeled, sliced and chopped
- 1 clove garlic, minced
- 6 slices bacon, cooked and chopped
- 6 medium red potatoes, thinly sliced
- 2 15-ounce cans stewed tomatoes, chopped
- 2 quarts fish stock or low sodium chicken stock
- salt and pepper
- 2 cups heavy cream

DIRECTIONS
In a large dutch oven or stockpot, melt the butter. Add the onion and garlic and sauté over low heat until the onions are translucent. Add the tomatoes, stock, bacon and potatoes. Increase the heat to medium and cook until the potatoes are tender. Adjust seasoning with salt and pepper to taste and add the fish. Continue cooking until the fish flakes. Stir in the cream and serve.

THIS IS A RUSTIC CHUNKY SOUP, COMFORT FOOD AT ITS BEST. FOR A MORE FORMAL PRESENTATION, PURÉE THE SOUP IN A FOOD PROCESSOR AND SERVE GARNISHED WITH FRESHLY GRATED CHEESE AND CROUTONS.

HOT AND SOUR FISH SOUP

SERVES 4

INGREDIENTS

- 1 pound boneless, skinless catfish fillets, cut into 1-inch pieces
- 2 medium zucchini, thinly sliced
- 1 jalapeño pepper, seeded and finely chopped
- 1 tablespoon olive oil
- 1 large onion, peeled, sliced and chopped
- 1 teaspoon red Thai curry paste
- 1 package frozen baby peas, thawed
- 2 teaspoons lime juice
- 4 tablespoons hoisin sauce
- 2 packages chicken-flavored ramen noodles
- 2 tablespoons Thai fish sauce

THIS MAKES A GREAT DIET MEAL—VERY LOW IN CALORIES. THAI CURRIES AND HOISIN ARE AVAILABLE AT MOST LARGE SUPERMARKETS.

DIRECTIONS

Cook the ramen noodles according to package directions. Keep warm.

Heat the oil in a large sauté pan or wok and stir-fry the onion until opaque. Stir in the curry paste, jalapeño pepper, zucchini and peas. Reduce heat to medium-low and stir-fry for 3–5 minutes or until zucchini is just cooked. Stir in the catfish, lime juice, hoisin sauce, fish sauce and 2 cups of the noodle broth. Bring to a boil, reduce the heat to low and simmer until the fish is cooked, about 3–5 minutes.

Divide the warm noodles among 4 serving bowls and top with equal portions of the soup.

PAN FISH, POTATO AND CORN CHOWDER

SERVES 6

INGREDIENTS

- 1 pound boneless, skinless crappie fillets, cut into 1-inch pieces
- 2 tablespoons vegetable oil
- ½ cup onion, chopped
- 2 cups water
- 2 large potatoes, peeled and diced
- salt and pepper to taste
- 2–3 cups milk
- 1 12-ounce can whole-kernel corn
- 1 cup light cream or evaporated milk
- chopped parsley or chopped green onion for garnish
- paprika

IF YOU LIKE A SWEET HEAVIER-BODIED CHOWDER, USE CREAMED CORN.

DIRECTIONS

Heat oil in a large heavy pot and lightly sauté the onion. Add water, potatoes, salt and pepper and bring to a simmer. Cook covered for 15 minutes (adding water if necessary), or until potatoes are tender. Add milk, corn and the fish and return to a simmer for 10 minutes or until fish is firm and cooked. Remove from the heat.

Stir in the cream and serve garnished with parsley or green onion and a sprinkling of paprika.

BAYOU FISH STEW

SERVES 4-6

INGREDIENTS

- 2 pounds boneless, skinless bluegill fillets
- 2 tablespoons seasoning salt
- ⅓ cup malt vinegar
- ¾ cup flour, seasoned with ¼ teaspoon white pepper
- 3 tablespoons vegetable oil
- 2 tablespoons olive oil
- 2 tablespoons butter
- 1 medium onion, peeled, sliced and finely chopped
- 1 red bell pepper, seeded, sliced and finely chopped
- 1 green bell pepper, seeded, sliced and finely chopped
- 1 jalapeño pepper, seeded and finely chopped
- 1 tablespoon minced garlic
- 1 15-ounce can stewed tomatoes, chopped
- 2½ cups low sodium chicken stock
- 2 tablespoons Thai fish sauce

TRUE COMFORT FOOD—GREAT FOR THE FAMILY OR A FORMAL DINNER PARTY.

DIRECTIONS

Dust the bluegill fillets with seasoning salt and place in a glass dish. Sprinkle with malt vinegar. Cover with plastic wrap and refrigerate overnight.

Remove the fillets from the glass dish and dry on paper towels. Place the flour and pepper in a large plastic bag and shake to mix. Coat fish fillets with the flour mixture.

In a large fry pan, heat the oil and fry the fillets, in batches, for 5 minutes or until golden brown. Remove and drain on paper towel.

In a large sauté pan, heat the butter and olive oil. Add the red and green peppers and garlic and stir-fry for 4–5 minutes. Add the tomatoes and jalapeño pepper and simmer 5 minutes. Stir in the chicken stock and fish sauce. Add the bluegill fillets and simmer until the stock has reduced by one-half. Serve with steamed white rice.

BASS-STUFFED SPINACH ROLLS IN SOUP

SERVES 4

INGREDIENTS
- 8 large fresh spinach leaves
- 1 cup cooked flaked bass
- 1 cup cooked rice
- 1 tablespoon lemon juice
- 2 tablespoons minced onion
- ½ teaspoon grated lemon rind
- 1 egg, beaten
- ⅛ teaspoon granulated garlic
- 2 or 3 drops Tabasco sauce
- 4 cups fish or chicken stock
- salt and pepper to taste
- 1 cup heavy cream (optional)
- paprika
- chopped parsley

TO ADD BODY TO YOUR STOCK, ADD A CAN OF CONDENSED CREAM OF CELERY SOUP WHEN YOU ADJUST THE SEASONING.

DIRECTIONS
Blanch spinach leaves in hot water to make leaf flexible.

Combine fish, rice, lemon juice, lemon rind, beaten egg, granulated garlic and Tabasco sauce. Divide into 8 portions and place each in the center of a spinach leaf. Fold two sides of the leaf over the filling, roll up and fasten with a toothpick. Place in a large heavy pot and cover with the fish or chicken stock. Bring to a simmer, cover and cook for 30 minutes. Remove the spinach rolls to a heated bowl. Cover and set aside.

Remove the pot with the stock from the heat. Season with salt and pepper and stir in the cream. Pour into bowls and place 2 spinach rolls in each bowl, garnishing with paprika and chopped parsley.

INDIAN FISH STEW

SERVES 4-6

INGREDIENTS

- 2 pounds boneless, skinless bass fillets
- 1½ cups low sodium chicken stock
- 2 tablespoons Thai fish sauce
- 3 medium potatoes, peeled and cut into 1-inch cubes
- 1 can stewed tomatoes, chopped
- 1 medium onion, peeled, sliced and chopped
- 1 red bell pepper, seeded and thinly sliced
- 1 green bell pepper, seeded and thinly sliced
- 2 teaspoons minced garlic
- 1 jalapeño pepper, seeded and finely chopped
- 1 bay leaf
- ½ teaspoon salt
- 1 teaspoon ground cumin
- 1 teaspoon ground coriander
- 1 teaspoon chili powder
- 2 tablespoons vegetable oil

SERVE WITH WARM PITA BREAD AND YOU'LL FEEL LIKE YOU'RE IN CALCUTTA.

DIRECTIONS

In a large sauté pan, heat the vegetable oil over medium heat. Add the onion, red and green peppers, garlic, jalapeño pepper and bay leaf. Cook, stirring occasionally, until the onion has browned, 5–6 minutes. Add the salt, cumin, coriander and chili powder and cook 4–5 minutes, being careful not to burn.

Stir in the tomatoes, potatoes, chicken stock and fish sauce. Bring to a boil, reduce heat and simmer 10 minutes. Add the bass fillets and simmer until tender. Serve over steamed rice.

BASIC FISH STOCK

INGREDIENTS

- 3–4 pounds fish heads, bone and fins from lean fish (avoid oily fish like salmon and trout)
- 4 tablespoons olive oil
- 1 large onion, thinly sliced
- 3 stalks celery, thinly sliced
- 4 carrots, peeled and thinly sliced
- 1 fennel bulb and fronds, thinly sliced
- 1 bunch parsley, chopped
- 2 inch piece of ginger, peeled and thinly sliced
- 3 whole bay leaves
- 2 garlic cloves, crushed
- 1 teaspoon dried thyme
- 1 teaspoon dried rosemary
- 2 cups white wine
- cold water
- celery salt

FREEZE SOME OF THE STOCK IN ICE CUBE TRAYS
FOR RECPIES CALLING FOR A SMALL AMOUNT OF
THE STOCK. 1 CUBE EQUALS ABOUT 1/4 CUP.

DIRECTIONS

Wash the fish heads, bones and fins under cold water. Remove and discard the gills as they will make the stock taste bitter.

In a tall stockpot, heat the olive oil on high. Add the fish heads, bones and fins and reduce the heat to medium. Stir for 5–6 minutes or until slightly browned. Add the vegetables and continue to cook until the onions are limp and opaque.

Stir in the wine, herbs and enough cold water to cover everything by 2 inches. Bring the stock to a simmer. Do not boil or the stock will turn cloudy. Simmer for 60 minutes.

Remove from the heat and allow to rest for 20–30 minutes. Strain the stock through a mesh strainer lined with cheesecloth or a basket-type coffee filter. If using a coffee filter, gently stir the stock in the strainer to speed the straining process. Discard all the filtered material. Add celery salt to the stock as desired.

After the stock has cooled, pour into 1-quart containers, leaving 1 inch for expansion. Cover and freeze. Yields about 3½ quarts.

HENRY'S BOUILLABAISSE

INGREDIENTS

- 12 ounces boneless, skinless catfish fillets, cut into 1½-inch pieces
- 12 ounces boneless, skinless salmon fillets, cut into 1½-inch pieces
- 12 ounces crayfish tails, cooked and peeled
- 4 ounces spicy chorizo sausage, thinly sliced
- ¼ cup olive oil
- 2 tablespoons butter
- 1 medium onion, peeled, quartered and thinly sliced
- 2 medium carrots, peeled and thinly sliced
- 1 fennel bulb, trimmed of any yellow or brown outside stalks, cut in half and thinly sliced (reserve fronds for garnish)
- 1 15-ounce can stewed tomatoes, chopped
- 1 medium zucchini, quartered and sliced
- 5 cups low sodium chicken stock

DIRECTIONS

In a 4-quart stockpot, heat the oil. Add the onion, fennel and carrots. Reduce heat to medium and cook until the carrots are tender. Add the butter and stir in the zucchini, tomatoes and chicken stock. Bring to a boil, reduce heat to medium and add the catfish, salmon, crayfish and chorizo sausage. Cover and simmer 10–15 minutes or until the fish is cooked.

Serve over steamed rice and garnish with chopped fennel fronds.

IF YOU DON'T CARE FOR AN ANISE FLAVOR, SUBSTITUTE CELERY FOR THE FENNEL AND USE CHOPPED PARSLEY FOR A GARNISH.

ENTRÉES

GRILLED PIKE BREW BITES

SERVES 4-6

INGREDIENTS

- 2 pounds boneless, skinless pike fillets
- 1 tablespoon olive oil
- 2 tablespoons garlic, minced
- 1 teaspoon dehydrated minced onion
- ½ teaspoon dill weed
- ¼ teaspoon celery salt
- ⅛ teaspoon black pepper
- 1 cup beer
- 10" bamboo skewers
- melted butter
- lemon wedges

IF BEER IS NOT YOUR THING, TRY 1 CUP ORANGE JUICE, ENHANCED WITH 2 OUNCES OF DARK RUM.

DIRECTIONS

Cut fillets into 1-inch strips crosswise. Thread several strips accordion style on 10" bamboo skewers. Arrange skewers in a single layer in a baking dish.

Combine remaining ingredients and pour over fish, turning skewers to coat. Cover with plastic warp and refrigerate at least 8 hours.

Spray your grill with non-stick vegetable spray. Heat to medium-high. Drain and discard the marinade. Arrange the skewers on grill. Cover and cook 3 minutes. Turn skewers, cover and continue grilling for 3–4 minutes or until fish is firm and begins to flake. Serve with melted butter and lemon wedges.

ARKANSAS STYLE PAN FISH

SERVES 4-6

INGREDIENTS
- 2 pounds crappie fillets
- 1 cup cornmeal
- 1 cup pecan pieces
- 1 cup seasoned breadcrumbs
- ¼ teaspoon salt
- dash of cayenne pepper
- 2 large eggs, well beaten

DIRECTIONS
Place the cornmeal, pecans, salt, cayenne pepper and breadcrumbs in a food processor. Process until very fine. Dip the fillets in the egg and then the meal mixture.

Heat frying oil to 375 degrees. Fry several pieces of fish at a time until golden brown. Drain on a paper towel and keep warm in a 200 degree oven until ready to serve.

THIS COATING MIXTURE WORKS WELL FOR ALL KINDS OF FISH. MAKE EXTRA AND STORE IN AN AIRTIGHT CONTAINER OR BAGS IN THE FREEZER.

BROILED BASS WITH LEMON BUTTER SAUCE

SERVES 4

INGREDIENTS
- 1½ pounds bass fillets, seasoned with salt and pepper
- 1 stick unsalted butter
- 3 tablespoons lemon juice
- ½ teaspoon grated orange zest
- ½ teaspoon grated lemon zest
- salt and white pepper

DIRECTIONS
In a medium saucepan, melt the butter and stir in the lemon juice and citrus zests. Season with salt and pepper to taste. Cover and keep warm.

Place the bass fillets, skin side down on a well-oiled broiler pan and broil about 3 inches below the heat source. Brush occasionally with the sauce. The fish is done when it flakes.

Garnish with orange and lemon slices and serve butter sauce on the side.

WHEN BROILING FISH, ALWAYS LEAVE THE
SKIN ON THE FILLETS. IT WILL AID IN
REMOVING THE FILLETS FROM THE PAN.

PERCH AND BACON SOUFFLÉ

INGREDIENTS

- 1 pound boneless, skinless perch fillets
- ½ cup milk
- ½ cup heavy cream
- 1 cup water
- 2 packages four cheese dehydrated mashed potatoes
- 1 teaspoon minced garlic
- 3 eggs, separated
- zest and juice of one small lemon
- 4 ounces bacon, cooked and crumbled
- 2 ounces grated sharp cheddar cheese

LIGHT, FLUFFY AND
SO VERY EASY—
YOUR GUESTS WILL
BE IMPRESSED.

DIRECTIONS

In a large saucepan, mix together the milk, cream and water. Bring the mixture to a boil, stirring constantly. Add the perch fillets, reduce heat to low and cook for 10–12 minutes or until the fish flakes. Drain, reserving the liquid, and place fish in a bowl.

Prepare the mashed potatoes according to package directions, using the reserved milk mixture. Mix in the garlic, egg yolks, lemon zest and juice.

Flake the fish and gently mix into the mashed potato mixture along with the crumbled bacon.

Beat the egg whites with a whisk or electric mixer, until stiff. Fold egg whites into the fish and potato mixture.

Spoon the mixture into 4 individual 10-ounce soufflé dishes or 1 large soufflé dish. Sprinkle the grated cheese on top and bake in a preheated 400 degree oven for 25–30 minutes or until the top is golden brown and the soufflé is firm to the touch.

BASS AND PASTA IN PARSLEY CREAM SAUCE

SERVES 4

INGREDIENTS
- 1 pound boneless, skinless bass fillets, cut into bite-size pieces
- 1 medium onion, peeled, sliced and coarsely chopped
- 4 tablespoons butter
- 1½ cups heavy cream
- 3 tablespoons fresh parsley, chopped
- salt and pepper to taste
- 8 ounces dry pasta shells, cooked according to package directions
- 1 cup shredded provolone cheese

DIRECTIONS
Melt the butter in a large sauté pan. Add the onion and stir-fry until opaque. Add the cream and bass pieces. Simmer for 5 minutes or until the fish begins to flake. Adjust seasoning with salt and pepper. Add cooked pasta shells, cheese and parsley, toss to combine. Continue cooking 2–3 minutes or until cheese begins to melt. Transfer to a heated serving bowl and serve immediately.

FOR ADDED FLAVOR, SPRINKLE WITH
TOASTED ALMONDS OR PECANS.

CRISPY PERCH

INGREDIENTS
- 8 perch fillets
- 1 package Shake 'N Bake for Chicken
- 2 tablespoons chopped parsley

DIRECTIONS
Butter a 1½-quart baking dish. Cover bottom of the dish with the parsley. Apply breading to the fish according to package directions and place perch in the baking dish.

Bake at 325 degrees for 10–15 minutes or until the golden brown.

A SIMPLE ACCOMPANIMENT TO THIS DISH IS OVEN BAKED HOME FRIES. BUTTER A 1-QUART BAKING DISH. ADD 3 MEDIUM BAKING POTATOES SLICED 3/8 INCH THICK. SEASON WITH SALT AND PEPPER AND DOT WITH BUTTER. BAKE UNCOVERED IN A 325 DEGREE OVEN FOR 20-30 MINUTES OR UNTIL GOLDEN BROWN AND FORK TENDER.

SUCKER BURGERS WITH PEPPER AND ONION

SERVES 6

INGREDIENTS

- 3 cups cooked sucker, flaked
- 1 cup finely processed cracker crumbs
- 2 large eggs, beaten
- ½ cup green pepper, chopped
- ½ cup onion, chopped
- ¼ cup butter
- 4 slices bacon, chopped
- salt and pepper to taste
- canola oil

DIRECTIONS

In a medium pan, melt the butter and sauté the green pepper and onion for 3–4 minutes.

In a large bowl, mix all ingredients. Shape into 6 equal burger patties. Sauté in canola oil until browned on both sides and cooked through.

MAKE THESE BURGERS AHEAD AND FREEZE—
MAKES A GREAT QUICK MEAL OR HEALTHY SNACK.

ITALIAN WALLEYE

SERVES 4

INGREDIENTS

- 4 8-ounce boneless, skinless walleye fillets
- 4 small baking potatoes, sliced
- 4 tablespoons olive oil
- 4 bay leaves
- 4 slices bacon
- 2 small onions, chopped
- 1 15-ounce can stewed tomatoes, chopped
- 24 green olives, pitted
- 2 tablespoons fresh parsley, chopped
- ½ cup dry white wine
- freshly ground pepper to taste

THE PERFECT AT-HOME
CAMPFIRE MEAL.

DIRECTIONS

Place 1 tablespoon of olive oil and 1 sliced potato in the center of a sheet of heavy duty aluminum foil. Place a walleye fillet on top of the potato. Place on the walleye, 1 bay leaf, 1 slice of bacon and ¼ of the onion, tomatoes and olives. Sprinkle with parsley and moisten with white wine and pepper to taste. Fold over and seal the foil to make a packet.

Repeat this process with the remaining 3 walleye fillets. Cook in the center of a 350 degree oven or covered grill for 12–15 minutes. Larger fillets may require more time. Serve immediately with steamed rice and fresh vegetables.

BASS FILLETS WITH ORANGE TOMATO SAUCE

SERVES 4-6

INGREDIENTS

- 2 pounds bass fillets, cut into 4–6 pieces
- ¼ cup flour
- ⅛ teaspoon ground cumin
- 1 tablespoon butter
- 2 tablespoons olive oil
- 1 medium onion, sliced and chopped
- 2 teaspoons minced garlic
- 1 15-ounce can stewed tomatoes, puréed in a food processor or blender
- ½ cup fresh orange juice
- zest from ½ orange

SAUCES WITH CITRUS JUICE SPARK UP THE FLAVOR OF TYPICALLY PLAIN-FLAVORED WHITE FRESHWATER FISH.

DIRECTIONS

Place the flour and cumin in a plastic bag and shake to mix. Add the bass fillets in batches, to coat. Shake off excess flour.

In a large sauté or fry pan, heat the butter and 1 tablespoon of the olive oil. Working in batches if necessary, fry the fillets for 3 minutes on each side, or until golden brown and the fish flakes with a fork. Transfer to a serving platter, cover with foil and keep warm.

Add the remaining olive oil to the pan. Stir in the onion and garlic and cook for 4–5 minutes or until the onion is translucent but not browned.

Stir in the tomato purée, orange juice and orange zest. Bring to a boil, reduce heat to medium-low and stir until thickened.

Garnish the bass fillets with orange wedges. Serve the sauce on the side.

POACHED WALLEYE

SERVES 2

INGREDIENTS
* 1 2-pound dressed walleye, with the head left on
* 2 quarts chicken broth
* 1 bottle clam juice

DIRECTIONS
Place fish in a fish poacher or in the center of a deep heavy-duty baking pan, leaving at least 1 inch of space on all sides. In a saucepan, bring the broth and clam juice to a fast boil and pour over the fish. Cover tightly with foil. In 10–20 minutes, depending on the thickness of the fish, remove the foil and test the fish for doneness. When done, it will flake easily. If additional poaching time is needed, reheat the broth. The internal temperature should be 165 degrees.

Remove the fish from the poaching liquid and serve immediately with melted butter and lemon wedges.

IF USING A BAKING PAN FOR POACHING,
PLACE THE WALLEYE ON CHEESECLOTH TO
AID IN REMOVING THE FISH FROM THE PAN.

SUCKER JAMBALAYA

SERVES 4

INGREDIENTS

* 1 pound boneless, skinless sucker fillets cut into 1-inch pieces
* 6 slices bacon, chopped
* ½ cup onion, chopped
* 1½ teaspoons garlic, chopped
* 1 medium green pepper, seeded and chopped
* 1 15-ounce can stewed tomatoes
* 2 cups low-sodium chicken stock
* salt and pepper to taste
* ¼ teaspoon chili powder (use more or less to taste)
* ⅛ teaspoon dried basil
* 1 teaspoon worcestershire sauce
* 1 cup rice
* ½ cup andouille sausage, diced

DIRECTIONS

Simmer the sucker in water to cover for 5–10 minutes or until firm and fully cooked. Drain, cover and keep warm.

In a heavy saucepan, fry the bacon. Add onion, garlic and green pepper and sauté lightly in the bacon fat. Add chicken stock, tomatoes, seasonings and rice. Bring to a boil, lower heat, cover and simmer, stirring frequently, until the rice is tender. Most of the liquid should be absorbed by the rice. Add the sucker, sausage and water, if necessary, for the last few minutes of cooking. Stir and serve.

TO STRETCH THIS RECIPE, ADD RICE—BE SURE TO ADD
LIQUID (WATER OR TOMATO JUICE) AS WELL.

LAKE TROUT WITH HONEY WINE SAUCE

SERVES 4-6

INGREDIENTS
- 1½ pounds lake trout fillets
- salt and pepper
- 1 stick unsalted butter
- 1½ tablespoons honey
- 1½ tablespoons white wine
- 1 teaspoon lemon juice
- 1 teaspoon teriyaki sauce

DIRECTIONS
In a medium saucepan, melt the butter and stir in the honey, wine, lemon juice and teriyaki sauce. Cover and keep warm

Season trout fillets with salt and pepper to taste. Place the fillets on an oiled broiler pan and broil about 3 inches below the heat source, brushing occasionally with the butter sauce. The fish is done when it flakes.

Garnish with lemon slices and serve the sauce on the side.

THE TIME FOR BROILING VARIES ACCORDING TO THE THICKNESS OF THE FILLETS, FROM ABOUT 3 MINUTES FOR A 3/8-INCH FILLET TO ABOUT 15 MINUTES FOR A 1 1/2-INCH THICK FILLET.

WALLEYE BALLS IN TOMATO SAUCE

SERVES 4-6

INGREDIENTS
- 2 pounds boneless, skinless walleye fillets, cut into 1m-inch chunks
- 1 cup fresh whole wheat breadcrumbs
- ¼ cup green onion, minced
- 2 15-ounce cans stewed tomatoes, chopped
- 2 cups fish stock or low sodium chicken stock
- 1 tablespoon Thai fish sauce
- ¼ pound button mushrooms, sliced (optional)
- ½ teaspoon crushed Italian seasoning
- salt and pepper to taste

DIRECTIONS
Place the walleye chunks in a food processor bowl fitted with a stainless steel blade. Pulse chop 2–3 times. Add the breadcrumbs and green onion, and pulse chop until well blended. Divide the mixture into 32 portions and mold into balls.

In a large saucepan, add the tomatoes, stock, fish sauce, mushrooms, Italian seasoning and salt and pepper to taste. Bring to a boil over medium heat. Add the walleye balls. Cover and simmer 10–12 minutes until cooked. Serve over pasta or with vegetables and a starch.

FOR A UNIQUE APPETIZER,
PREPARE 1/2 OUNCE PORTIONS.

BAKED PAN FISH LOUISIANA STYLE

SERVES 4

INGREDIENTS

- 2 pounds boneless, skinless pan fish fillets
- 2 tablespoons olive oil
- 2 tablespoons butter
- 1 medium onion, peeled, sliced and cut in half
- 2 teaspoons minced garlic
- 1 large red bell pepper, seeded and thinly sliced
- 1 large green bell pepper, seeded and thinly sliced
- 1 15-ounce can stewed tomatoes, chopped
- 1 tablespoon capers, chopped
- 1 tablespoon fresh basil, minced
- ¼ cup fine cracker meal
- ¼ cup fresh grated Romano cheese

THIS IS A GOOD
WAY TO USE UP
THE LAST OF
THOSE PAN FISH
SLEEPING IN
THE FREEZER.

DIRECTIONS

In a large sauté pan, heat the oil and butter over low heat. Add the garlic and onion and stir-fry until the onion is tender. Add the peppers, tomatoes, capers and basil. Increase the heat to medium and simmer for 10 minutes. Remove from the heat.

Butter the bottom and sides of a baking dish. Arrange the fish in the dish and cover with the tomato and pepper mixture. Bake in a 350 degree oven for 15–20 minutes. Cover with the cracker meal and top with the grated cheese. Return to the oven for 10–12 minutes or until golden brown. Serve with steamed vegetables and garlic bread with hot sauce on the side.

OVEN FRIED BASS WITH TARTER SAUCE

SERVES 4

INGREDIENTS
- 4 6-oz boneless, skinless bass fillets
- ½ cup dried breadcrumbs
- ½ cup cracker crumbs
- 2 tablespoons grated Parmesan cheese
- ½ teaspoon dried oregano
- ½ cup milk
- 3 tablespoons melted butter

TARTER SAUCE
- 1 cup mayonnaise
- 2 teaspoons dijon mustard
- 1 tablespoon capers, chopped
- 1 tablespoon sweet pickle relish
- 2 teaspoons fresh parsley, chopped
- 2 teaspoons fresh chives, chopped
- 2 teaspoons fresh tarragon, chopped
- 1 teaspoon curry powder

ALL THE FLAVOR
OF THE CLASSIC,
BUT WITHOUT
DEEP FRYING.

DIRECTIONS

Preheat oven to 325 degrees.

In a medium bowl, combine all tarter sauce ingredients and mix thoroughly. Cover and refrigerate.

In a food processor bowl fitted with a stainless steel blade, combine the breadcrumbs, cracker crumbs, Parmesan cheese and dried oregano. Pulse chop and then process until completely blended, about 30 seconds. Transfer this mixture to a plastic bag.

Prepare a 9"x12" baking dish with non-stick spray.

Pour the milk into a medium bowl. Dip the bass fillets in the milk and then coat with the breading mixture in the plastic bag.

Arrange the fillets in the baking dish and drizzle with the melted butter. Bake for 10–15 minutes. The fillets should be golden brown and flake with a fork. Serve with the tarter sauce.

WALLEYE LASAGNA

SERVES 4-6

INGREDIENTS

- 1 pound boneless, skinless walleye fillets
- 12 ounces oven-ready lasagna noodles
- 2 tablespoons butter
- 1 medium onion, peeled, sliced and chopped
- 2 teaspoons garlic, minced
- 6 ounces mushrooms, sliced
- 2 packages Knorr White Sauce mix, prepared according to package directions
- ⅓ cup fresh parsley, chopped
- 1 package frozen baby peas, thawed
- 4 ounces mozzarella cheese, grated
- 4 ounces provolone cheese, grated
- 2 sweet red peppers, seeded and cut into julienne strips
- 2 ounces grated Parmesan cheese

IF YOU PREFER A CHEESIER FLAVOR, REPLACE THE MOZZARELLA CHEESE WITH GRATED SHARP CHEDDAR.

DIRECTIONS

Prepare lasagna noodles according to package directions. Drain and cover to keep moist. Cook the walleye in the microwave on high, until just set. Let cool to room temperature.

In a large saucepan, melt the butter. Add the onion and sauté for 3–4 minutes or until soft. Add the mushrooms and garlic. Cook for an additional 3–4 minutes, stirring occasionally. Stir in the white sauce, peas and parsley. Season to taste with salt and pepper.

Spoon a thin layer of sauce over the bottom of a 9"x12" baking dish. Cover with a layer of lasagna noodles, then walleye, sauce, lasagna noodles, walleye, sauce, lasagna noodles, sauce and Parmesan cheese.

Bake in a preheated 325 degree oven for 40–50 minutes or until bubbly and the top is golden brown. Remove from the oven and let set for 15 minutes before serving.

BAKED PIKE LOAF

INGREDIENTS

- 1½ pounds boneless, skinless pike fillets, cut into 1-inch by 2-inch pieces
- 2 cups baked potatoes, thinly sliced
- ¼ teaspoon salt
- ⅛ teaspoon white pepper
- 2 tablespoons butter, softened
- 2 eggs, well beaten
- 1 cup seasoned breadcrumbs
- ⅛ teaspoon nutmeg
- ½ cup heavy cream
- 2 tablespoons fresh parsley, chopped

DIRECTIONS

Butter the bottom of a 9"x15" inch loaf pan. Season the potatoes with salt and pepper and place the slices in overlapping layers on the bottom of the pan.

Mix the eggs with the cream and nutmeg. Fold in the breadcrumbs and the fish. Place the mixture on top of the potatoes, pressing down to remove any air. Cover with foil and bake in a 350 degree oven for 40–50 minutes or until the egg and cream mixture has set.

Loosen the edges with a butter knife and invert on a warm serving platter. Garnish with chopped parsley.

A SIMPLE TARTAR SAUCE CAN BE MADE BY MIXING 1 CUP OF MAYONNAISE WITH 1 TABLESPOON DILL RELISH, 1 TABLESPOON SWEET RELISH AND 1/2 TEASPOON PAPRIKA.

HERBED WALLEYE

SERVES 4

INGREDIENTS

- 1 pound boneless, skinless walleye fillets
- 3 tablespoons butter
- 1 teaspoon salt
- dash of white pepper
- 1 bay leaf
- ½ teaspoon granulated garlic
- ¼ teaspoon thyme
- ½ cup onion, thinly sliced
- ¾ cup half & half

DIRECTIONS

Place fish fillets in a buttered rectangular baking dish. Dot with butter and sprinkle with pepper, granulated garlic and thyme. Add the bay leaf and arrange onion rings over the top. Pour half & half over the fish. Bake uncovered in a 350 degree oven 12–20 minutes or until the internal temperature of the fish is 140 degrees and the fish flakes with a fork.

COOKING FISH IN MILK IS A VERY OLD TECHNIQUE
THAT PRODUCES SURPRISING RESULTS—
FISH THAT DOESN'T TASTE FISHY.

PAN FISH AND RICE PIE

SERVES 4

INGREDIENTS

- ¾ pound boneless, skinless crappie fillets
- double crust pie pastry
- 1¼ cups cooked rice
- 2 tablespoons minced onion
- 2 tablespoons green onion, seeded and diced
- ¼ cup grated cheddar cheese
- 3 tablespoons butter
- 2 large eggs, well beaten

THIS DISH WILL ADD
SOMETHING SPECIAL TO
A BREAKFAST BUFFET.

DIRECTIONS

Grease a pie pan and place a round of pie pastry in the bottom. Add ½ of the rice and cheese and top with the crappie fillets. Dot the fish with butter and add the onion and green pepper. Top with the remaining rice and cheese and the beaten eggs. Top with the remaining round of pie pastry, seal the edges and cut 2 vents in the top. Bake on a cookie sheet in the center of a 400 degree oven for 45 minutes or until the crust is lightly browned. Let the pie rest for 30 minutes before serving.

CHEESY BAKED PERCH

SERVES 4

INGREDIENTS

- 8 medium whole dressed perch, head on
- 4 tablespoons olive oil
- pinch of salt
- pinch of white pepper
- 2 teaspoons minced garlic
- 1 cup grated Parmesan and Romano cheeses
- 1 teaspoon Italian seasoning
- 2 Ritz crackers

YOU CAN SUBSTITUTE PERCH FILLETS IN THIS RECIPE—ALLOW 4 PER PERSON AND ADJUST THE BAKING TIME TO 8-10 MINUTES.

DIRECTIONS

In a small bowl, mix together the olive oil, salt, pepper and garlic.

Place the perch in a single layer in a baking dish or pan. Pour the garlic and oil mixture over the perch, turning to coat all sides. Let the fish marinate in the refrigerator for 20–30 minutes.

Place the crackers, cheese and Italian seasoning in a food processor bowl fitted with a stainless steel blade and process until finely chopped. Place this mixture in a large plastic bag.

Remove fish from the marinade an place on a paper towel to drain excess oil. Place the fish, one at a time, in the bag with the breading mixture and shake to coat. Place the coated fish in a single layer on an oiled baking sheet.

Bake at 350 degrees for 15–20 minutes or until fish is brown and flakes with a fork.

BACON WRAPPED BASS KABOBS

INGREDIENTS
- 24 pieces bass fillet, cut into strips, 1 inch wide and 6 inches long
- 24 strips pre-cooked bacon
- 4 12-inch bamboo skewers

BASTING SAUCE
- 1 cup teriyaki sauce
- 1 tablespoon brown sugar
- ½ cup white wine
- ¼ teaspoon tarragon
- dash hot sauce

DIRECTIONS
Roll the bass strips into cylinders and wrap each with a bacon strip. Thread 6 cylinders onto each skewer.

In a 1-quart saucepan, mix together the basting sauce ingredients. Stir over low heat until the sugar is dissolved. Baste the kabobs. Place in an oiled skillet and cook over medium heat 4–5 minutes per side. Bass should be slightly opaque but firm. Serve with lemon wedges and basting sauce.

IF YOU DON'T THINK THE KABOBS ARE QUITE DONE,
MICROWAVE ON HIGH FOR 40 SECONDS—
BE SURE YOU ARE USING WOODEN SKEWERS.

LAKE TROUT BAKED IN GRAPE LEAVES WITH OLIVE SALSA

SERVES 4

INGREDIENTS

- 4 6-ounce boneless, skinless lake trout fillets
- 1 16-ounce jar grape leaves
- ½ cup couscous
- 1 small jar roasted red pepper or pimento
- 1 tablespoon chopped cilantro
- 1 tablespoon chopped parsley
- 1 tablespoon lemon zest, chopped
- 1 teaspoon minced garlic
- 1 teaspoon chopped basil
- 2 tablespoons olive oil
- salt and pepper
- 4 orange slices
- 1 cup dry white wine
- 4 ounces feta cheese with basil and tomato
- 1 cup shredded lettuce

OLIVE SALSA

- 2 tablespoons minced onion
- ¼ cup kalamata olives, pitted and chopped
- ¼ cup salad olives, pitted and chopped
- 3 tablespoons red wine vinegar
- 2 teaspoons chopped oregano
- ¼ cup olive oil

DIRECTIONS

Soak grape leaves in 1 cup hot water for 5 minutes. Remove, unfold and drain.

Place couscous in a bowl an stir in ½ cup boiling water. Cover and let rest for 5 minutes. Fluff with a fork. Add the red peppers, cilantro, parsley, lemon zest, garlic, basil and olive oil. Season with salt and pepper to taste.

Season the fillets with salt and pepper and top each with 2 tablespoons of the couscous and an orange slice. Wrap each fillet with grape leaves and place in a roasting pan. Brush with olive oil, add the wine, cover and bake at 325 degrees for 15–20 minutes, basting occasionally.

While the fish is baking, combine all salsa ingredients in a small bowl.

IF GRAPE LEAVES ARE NOT AVAILABLE, USE BUTTERED SQUARES
OF ALUMINUM FOIL TO FORM INDIVIDUAL BAKING PACKETS.

WALLEYE RAVIOLI

SERVES 4

INGREDIENTS

* 6 ounces boneless, skinless walleye fillets, diced
* grated rind of ½ orange and ½ lemon
* 1 garlic clove, minced
* 2 tablespoons roasted pistachio nuts, shelled
* 2 tablespoons fresh parsley, chopped
* 1 egg
* salt and pepper
* ¼ cup heavy cream
* 1 package wonton wrappers
* 1 egg, beaten
* 2 sticks butter
* 2 tablespoons fresh basil, chopped

FOR ADDED FLAVOR, SERVE WITH GRATED ROMANO CHEESE.

DIRECTIONS

Place the walleye, citrus rind, garlic, pistachios and parsley in a food processor, and pulse until finely chopped. Add the egg, cream and salt and pepper to taste. Process to form a thick purée. Transfer to a mixing bowl, cover and refrigerate.

Place 20 wonton wrappers on a clean work surface. Divide the filling among the wrappers. Paint the edges with beaten egg, and place a second wrapper on top. Pinch the edges to seal, removing as much air as possible.

In a small saucepan, melt the butter and add the basil. Remove from the heat and set aside.

Add 2 quarts of water to a large sauté pan. Bring to a simmer and poach the ravioli in small batches for 3–4 minutes or until they rise to the surface. Drain and dress with the butter and basil. Divide the ravioli among 4 plates and serve with additional butter and basil.

OVEN FRIED SMELT

INGREDIENTS

- 30 dressed smelt, head removed
- ¾ cup flour
- ¾ cup finely ground cornmeal
- 1 teaspoon celery salt
- ¼ teaspoon white pepper
- canola oil

DIRECTIONS

Mix together the flour, cornmeal, salt and pepper and place in a large plastic bag. Place the smelt in the bag and shake to coat.

Pour ⅛ inch canola oil into a shallow baking dish with 1" sides. Place the smelt in the pan, one at a time, and turn to coat all sides with the oil. Place the pan in the center of a 425 degree oven. Bake until golden brown, turning after the first 5–6 minutes.

OVEN FRYING IS ACCOMPLISHED WITH A MINIMAL AMOUNT OF OIL AND IS A CONVENIENT WAY TO COOK A LARGE AMOUNT OF FISH.

PAN FISH, PEAS AND PASTA CASSEROLE

SERVES 4-6

INGREDIENTS

- 2 cups crappie fillets, cooked and chunked
- 4 cups shell pasta, cooked
- 1 package frozen peas
- 2 cans condensed mushroom soup
- 1 cup heavy cream
- ⅛ teaspoon nutmeg
- cracker crumbs

FOR A DIFFERENT
FLAVOR, ADD A
LAYER OR TWO OF
SHREDDED SHARP
CHEDDAR CHEESE.

DIRECTIONS

Butter or oil an oven-proof casserole dish. Build several layers, beginning with pasta, then fish and peas. The top layer should be pasta.

Mix together the soup, cream and nutmeg. Pour over the top of the layered fish and pasta. Sprinkle the top with cracker crumbs. Bake in a 325 degree oven for 30–40 minutes or until the top is browned and the casserole is hot and bubbly.

CATFISH CURRY

INGREDIENTS

- 1 pound boneless, skinless catfish fillets, cut into 1-inch pieces
- 1 large onion, sliced
- 1 clove garlic, minced
- 2 teaspoons Thai yellow curry paste
- 1 teaspoon brown sugar
- salt to taste
- 1 15-ounce can coconut milk
- ½ tablespoon vegetable oil
- juice of ¼ lime or lemon
- cooked rice

DIRECTIONS

In a large fry pan, combine the catfish with garlic, curry paste, brown sugar, salt and half of the onion. Mix well, add coconut milk and simmer about 3 minutes or until the fish is cooked. Set aside. Heat oil in the fry pan and sauté the remaining onion. Add to the fish mixture, stir in lime juice and cook over low heat for 5 minutes. Serve over the cooked rice.

BEFORE ADDING THE CURRY PASTE, MIX IT WITH A SMALL
AMOUNT OF HOT WATER—IT WILL INCORPORATE WITH
THE OTHER INGREDIENTS MUCH BETTER THIS WAY.

CURRIED PERCH WITH CARROTS AND POTATOES

SERVES 4

INGREDIENTS

- 1 pound boneless perch fillets
- 2 medium potatoes, peeled and cut into ½-inch dice
- 3 medium carrots, peeled and cut into ¼-inch dice
- 3 green onions, finely sliced
- 2 tablespoons Thai fish sauce
- 2 13-ounce cans coconut milk
- 1½ tablespoons yellow Thai curry paste dissolved in 2 tablespoons hot water
- 2 teaspoons brown sugar
- 12 cherry tomatoes, stemmed and cut in half

IF YOU PREFER, SERVE OVER PASTA.

DIRECTIONS

Place the carrots and potatoes in a 2-quart saucepan, cover with water and bring to a boil. Cook until just tender, drain and set aside.

In a large sauté pan, heat the coconut milk over low heat. Stir in the curry paste and brown sugar.

Cut the perch into ½-inch diagonal strips. Add to the coconut mixture and simmer for 10 minutes. Stir in the potatoes, carrots, green onion, tomatoes and fish sauce. Continue to simmer for an additional 6–8 minutes. Serve over steamed rice, garnished with the cherry tomato halves.

WALLEYE AND CRAYFISH WITH ORZO PASTA

SERVES 4

INGREDIENTS

- ½ pound boneless, skinless walleye fillets, cut into 1-inch pieces
- ½ pound cooked crayfish tail meat, cut into 1-inch pieces
- 1 teaspoon garlic, minced
- 1 small onion, peeled, sliced and chopped
- 3 tablespoons butter
- 1 package frozen baby peas, thawed
- 4 cups low sodium chicken stock
- 1 tablespoon Thai fish sauce (optional)
- 2 cups uncooked orzo pasta

DIRECTIONS

In a 4-quart pot over medium heat, melt the butter. Add the onion and garlic. Cook until tender, being careful not to burn the garlic. Stir in the chicken stock and increase the heat to high. When the stock boils, stir in the orzo pasta, fish sauce and peas. Reduce heat to low, cover and simmer for 15 minutes or until the pasta has absorbed the liquid.

Stir in the walleye and crayfish. Cover and continue cooking for 5–10 minutes or until the walleye is cooked and the crayfish is heated through. Let stand for 5 minutes and transfer to a heated serving platter.

IF YOU LIKE RISOTTO BUT CAN'T STAND THE FUSS, THIS IS A SIMPLE ALTERNATIVE. EXPERIMENT—ADD YOU FAVORITE CHEESE TO CREATE A FABULOUS SIDE DISH FOR YOUR FAVORITE ENTRÉE.

PIKE, PASTA AND CHEESE LOAF

SERVES 4-6

INGREDIENTS

* 1 pound pike fillets, cooked and flaked
* 4 cups cooked shell pasta
* ¾ pound shredded sharp cheddar cheese
* 1 cup seasoned breadcrumbs
* 2 tablespoons melted butter
* 4 eggs, beaten
* ¾ cup heavy cream
* 1 tablespoon dehydrated onion
* 2 tablespoons pimiento, chopped
* 2 tablespoons green pepper, chopped
* ½ teaspoon salt
* ⅛ teaspoon white pepper

IF YOU'RE LOOKING FOR FEWER CALORIES, SUBSTITUTE COTTAGE CHEESE OR RICOTTA CHEESE FOR THE SHARP CHEDDAR AND 2% MILK FOR THE HEAVY CREAM.

DIRECTIONS

Mix ¼ cup breadcrumbs with the melted butter and set aside. Mix the remaining breadcrumbs with the flaked fish.

Butter an oven-proof casserole and begin layering with pasta, the pike and then the cheese. Do two layers of each ingredient and top with an additional layer of pasta.

Using an electric mixer, blend the remaining ingredients. Whip until completely blended. Pour over the layered casserole and top with the buttered breadcrumbs.

Bake in a 325 degree oven for 30–40 minutes or until custard has set and the top is golden brown.

GREEKTOWN SALMON WITH CUCUMBER SAUCE

SERVES 4

INGREDIENTS

- 4 6-ounce boneless, skinless salmon fillets
- 1 tablespoon Greek seasoning
- ½ cup plain yogurt
- 2 tablespoons olive oil
- dill sprigs for garnish

CUCUMBER SAUCE

- 2 cucumbers, peeled and seeded
- 2 tablespoons coarse salt
- 2 teaspoons minced garlic
- 1 cup plain yogurt
- 1 cup sour cream
- 3 tablespoons fresh dill, chopped
- 1 tablespoon lemon juice

SALTING THE CUCUMBERS REMOVES EXCESS MOISTURE AND IS A NECESSARY STEP FOR THIS DISH.

DIRECTIONS

Combine the yogurt with the Greek seasoning. Cover all sides of the salmon fillet with the yogurt mixture. Place in a sealable plastic bag and refrigerate at least 1 hour.

Heat a heavy skillet over high heat. Add the olive oil. Sear the fillets for 2 minutes. Place the fillets in a baking pan, seared side up, and bake in a 350 degree oven for 3–5 minutes. Garnish with the cucumber sauce and dill sprigs.

To prepare the Cucumber Sauce, grate the cucumbers and toss with garlic and salt. Transfer to a strainer set over a bowl. Refrigerate 2–3 hours.

Rinse the cucumber under cold water. Press with a spoon to remove excess moisture. Place in the center of a kitchen towel and squeeze to remove any remaining liquid.

In a medium bowl, mix together the yogurt, lemon juice, dill and sour cream. Stir in the cucumbers. Adjust with salt to taste if desired. Cover and refrigerate at least 1 hour before serving.

CREOLE CATFISH AND RICE CASSEROLE

SERVES 6

INGREDIENTS

- 1 pound boneless, skinless catfish fillets, cut into 1-inch pieces
- ½ cup bacon, chopped
- 1 cup onion, chopped
- 1 cup green pepper, seeded and chopped
- 4 cloves garlic, crushed and chopped
- 1 cup long grain white rice
- 3 cups stewed tomatoes, chopped
- 1 cup celery, chopped
- 1 cup fish stock
- 1 cup low sodium chicken stock
- salt, white pepper and cayenne pepper to taste

DIRECTIONS

Butter a 2-quart casserole dish and preheat the oven to 325 degrees.

In a heavy sauté pan, fry the bacon until crisp. Add the onion, green pepper and garlic. Sauté until the onion is translucent. Transfer to a large bowl and mix in the remaining ingredients. Transfer the mixture to the casserole dish. Bake for 45–60 minutes or until the rice is tender.

YOU'LL PROBABLY WANT TO GO EASY ON THE WHITE AND CAYENNE PEPPERS. SERVE HOT SAUCE ON THE SIDE TO ADD EXTRA FIRE.

SOBA NOODLES WITH PERCH

SERVES 4

INGREDIENTS

- 1 pound boneless perch fillets cut into 1-inch strips
- 6 ounces soba noodles
- 4 ounces shiitake mushrooms, stemmed and cut into thin strips
- 2 cloves garlic, minced
- 4 baby bok choy, quartered
- 2 green onions, diagonally sliced end-to-end
- 3 tablespoons vegetable oil
- 2 tablespoons toasted sesame oil
- 2 tablespoons rice wine
- 2 tablespoons teriyaki sauce
- ¼ cup cilantro leaves
- 1½ tablespoons toasted sesame seeds

DIRECTIONS

Prepare the soba noodles according to the package directions and keep warm (do not drain).

In a large sauté pan or wok, heat the oil. Add the mushrooms, garlic, green onion and bok choy and stir-fry for 2–3 minutes. Add the perch, sesame oil, rice wine and teriyaki sauce and continue to cook for 2–3 minutes or until perch is cooked (if too dry, add some of the noodle cooking liquid).

Drain the noodles and divide among 4 plates or bowls. Top with the perch and vegetables. Garnish with cilantro leaves and sesame seeds.

THIS IS A GREAT DISH IF YOU ARE DIETING. ADD CARROTS
OR CELERY FOR ADDITIONAL FIBER AND FLAVORS.

LAKE TROUT WITH STOUT SHEPHERD'S PIE

SERVES 4

INGREDIENTS

- 1½ pounds potatoes, peeled, cubed, cooked and mashed
- 1 pound boneless, skinless lake trout fillets
- 1 bay leaf
- 1 cup milk
- 1 cup Guinness stout
- 4 tablespoons butter
- 4 large leeks, sliced (white part only)
- 1½ cups mushrooms, sliced and chopped
- 2 tablespoons flour
- ½ teaspoon Colman's dry mustard
- 2 tablespoons fresh parsley, chopped
- 1 tablespoon lemon juice
- 2 hard boiled eggs, sliced and chopped
- salt and pepper
- 4 ounces grated cheddar cheese

TOASTED CRUSTY BREAD
AND YET ANOTHER PINT
OF STOUT COMPLETE
THIS DISH PERFECTLY.

DIRECTIONS

Melt the butter in a large sauté pan. Add the leeks and cook over medium heat until tender, about 10 minutes. Add the mushrooms and cook another 3–4 minutes. Stir in the flour to make a roux and remove the pan from the heat.

Place the trout fillets and bay leaf in a shallow pan, cover with milk and stout. Cover pan with foil and bake in a 325 degree oven for 20 minutes or until trout begins to flake. Remove the fillets from the baking dish and set aside. Discard the bay leaf.

Return the leek mixture to the stove. Over low heat, gradually stir in the cooking liquid and cook until thickened, about 10 minutes. Add the mustard, parsley, lemon juice, eggs and salt and pepper to taste. Flake the fish and add to the pan.

Spoon the mixture into a well-buttered baking dish. Top with the mashed potatoes. Using a fork, create a "hills and valleys" surface to encourage browning. Sprinkle the top with the cheddar cheese. Bake at 325 degrees until filling is bubbly and the top is crusty and browned.

ORIENTAL SMELT FRY WITH THAI HOT SAUCE

SERVES 6

INGREDIENTS
- 60 small smelt, dressed with head removed
- peanut or canola oil for frying

NAM PRIK (THAI HOT SAUCE)
- 10 cloves garlic, chopped
- 5 dried red chilies, chopped
- 1 tablespoon brown sugar
- 1 cup oriental fish sauce (nam pla)
- 1 cup lime juice
- 4 fresh jalapeño peppers, seeded and chopped
- 1 cup teriyaki sauce

DIRECTIONS
Prepare the sauce several days ahead of use. Mix the garlic, red chilies and brown sugar to a smooth paste. Slowly mix in the fish sauce and lime juice. Add the teriyaki and jalapeno peppers. Cover and refrigerate at least 1–2 days before serving. Leftover sauce will last for weeks under refrigeration.

In a wok, heat oil to 375 degrees. Fry the smelt, a few at a time, until nicely browned. Drain on a paper towel and place in a warm oven until ready to serve. Served with steamed vegetables and rice with the Nam prik on the side.

THE FLAVOR IN THIS DISH COMES FROM THE SAUCE WHICH IS THE THAI EQUIVALENT OF OUR TABLE CONDIMENTS. TO TONE DOWN THE HEAT, MIX 1/4 CUP NAM PRIK WITH 1 CUP MAYONNAISE.

PASTA WITH BLUEGILLS, PEAS AND ANCHOVIES

SERVES 4

INGREDIENTS
- 1½ pounds bluegill fillets, cooked and flaked
- 2 tablespoons olive oil
- 1 tablespoon butter
- 1 teaspoon minced garlic
- 1 15-oz can stewed tomatoes, puréed in a food processor
- 5–6 anchovy fillets, finely minced
- 1 package frozen baby peas, thawed
- salt and pepper
- 8 ounces dry penne or rigatoni pasta, cooked according to package directions (about 4 cups)
- 1 tablespoon fresh basil, thinly sliced

DIRECTIONS
Heat the oil and butter in a large sauté pan. Add the garlic and stir-fry for 1 minute. Stir in the anchovies, tomato purée and peas. Reduce heat to low, cover and simmer for 15–20 minutes.

Gently stir in the bluegill and basil and adjust seasoning to taste with salt and pepper. Refresh the cooked pasta in hot water. Drain and stir into the sauce. Arrange on a large serving platter or bowl. Garnish with basil and freshly grated cheese.

MOST PASTA CAN BE COOKED AHEAD OF TIME AND HELD IN WATER. TO SERVE, REFRESH IN HOT WATER AND DRAIN.

CATFISH KABOBS

SERVES 4

INGREDIENTS

* 1½ pounds boneless, skinless catfish fillets, cut into 1-inch cubes
* 12 strips bacon
* 2 small zucchini squash, cut into ½-inch slices
* 1 sweet red pepper, seeded and cut into 1-inch squares
* 10" bamboo skewers

MARINADE

* ⅓ cup olive oil
* zest of ½ lemon
* 3 tablespoons lemon juice
* 3 tablespoons white wine
* ¼ cup fresh dill, chopped
* 1 tablespoon honey
* salt and pepper

BEFORE STARTING YOUR GRILL, REMOVE THE COOKING GRATE AND TREAT WITH A NON-STICK COOKING SPRAY. REPLACE THE GRATE JUST BEFORE YOU START TO GRILL THE KABOBS—THEY'LL HAVE LESS TENDENCY TO STICK TO THE GRILL.

DIRECTIONS

Combine the marinade ingredients in a stainless steel bowl. Cover and set aside.

Cut bacon strips in half. Wrap each catfish cube with bacon. Thread a wrapped cube on a skewer followed by a pepper square and a squash slice. Build each skewer to 3 pieces of catfish, pepper and squash.

Place kabobs in a single layer in a shallow pan or dish. Add the marinade. Cover and refrigerate for at least 1 hour.

Grill the kabobs over medium heat for 3–4 minutes on each side, basting occasionally with the marinade. Serve with steamed rice.

BAKED PERCH WITH APRICOTS, DRIED CRANBERRIES AND OLIVES

SERVES 4

INGREDIENTS
- 2 pounds boneless, skinless perch fillets
- 3 dried apricots and 1 tablespoon dried cranberries, soaked for 2 hours in ⅓ cup cream sherry
- 1 stick butter
- ½ cup sliced kalamata olives
- 3 green onions, thinly sliced
- 1 cup heavy cream
- 2 cups white wine
- 1 cup clam juice

DIRECTIONS
Drain the apricots and cranberries. Chop the apricots to the same size as the cranberries.

Fold and layer the perch fillets in a buttered baking dish. Top with the apricots, cranberries, olives and green onion. Mix the wine and clam juice together and pour over the fillets. Cover with foil and bake in a 350 degree oven for 12–15 minutes.

Remove the foil and pour the cooking liquid into a saucepan. Return the fish to the oven to keep warm. Bring the cooking liquid to a boil and reduce by one-half. Reduce heat to low and whisk in the cream and butter. Pour sauce over the fish. Serve with steamed vegetables.

FRUIT, BALANCED WITH SALTY ITEMS LIKE OLIVES OR CAPERS, IMPARTS A SWEET/SOUR FLAVOR PROFILE TO THE FISH.

SMOKED SALMON IN CREAM SAUCE WITH RAMEN NOODLES

SERVES 4-6

INGREDIENTS

- 10 ounces skinless smoked salmon fillets, cut into thin strips
- 2 packages ramen chicken-flavored noodles, cooked according to package directions and kept warm
- 1 leek, white part only, cut into julienne strips
- 2 stalks celery hearts, cut into julienne strips
- 2 carrots, peeled and cut into julienne strips
- 4 tablespoons butter
- 1 cup noodle broth
- 4 ounces cream cheese
- 4 ounces mascarpone cheese
- fresh parsley, chopped

DIRECTIONS

In a large sauté pan, melt the butter. Add the leeks, celery and carrots. Stir-fry for 2–3 minutes. Add the noodle broth and bring to a boil. Reduce until most of the broth has evaporated. Remove from the heat and whisk in cream cheese and mascarpone. If mixture is too thick, add small amount of noodle broth.

Add the salmon. Drain the noodles and gently stir into the sauce. Transfer to a warm serving platter and garnish with fresh chopped parsley.

TO REDUCE THE SALT IN THIS DISH, USE ONLY HALF
THE SEASONING PACKAGES WITH THE NOODLES.

LEBANESE FISH WITH COUSCOUS

SERVES 4

INGREDIENTS
- 2 pounds boneless, skinless catfish fillets
- 2 tablespoons olive oil
- 3 cups fish or low sodium chicken stock
- 2 large onions, peeled, sliced and chopped
- ½ teaspoon ground cumin
- 3–4 saffron threads, soaked in 1 tablespoon hot water (optional)
- 4 ounces toasted pistachio nuts, coarsely chopped
- 1 cup couscous
- salt and pepper to taste

A FLAVORFUL SAUCE FOR THIS DISH IS 1/2 CUP SOUR CREAM MIXED WITH 1 1/2 TABLESPOONS DIJON MUSTARD, 1 TEASPOON HONEY AND 1/2 TEASPOON CHOPPED FRESH DILL.

MARINADE
- 1 tablespoon olive oil, mixed with the juice of 1 lemon

DIRECTIONS
Place the catfish in a shallow dish and add the marinade. Turn to coat well. Cover and refrigerate 30–40 minutes.

In a large sauté pan, heat the oil over medium heat and fry the onion until golden. Remove onion from the pan. Drain the fish and fry for 2 minutes on each side or until light brown. Add the onion, stock, cumin, saffron and the marinade. Bring to a boil, reduce heat to low and simmer 6–8 minutes.

Transfer the fish to a heated platter. Cover and keep warm.

Season the broth in the sauté pan to taste with salt and pepper. Bring to a boil, stir in the couscous, cover and remove from the heat. Let stand for 5–6 minutes. Fluff couscous with a fork. Divide among 4 dinner plates. Arrange a fish portion on top and sprinkle with pistachios. Garnish with parsley and serve immediately.

OVEN BAKED BLUEGILLS WITH BLEU CHEESE SAUCE

SERVES 4

INGREDIENTS
- 1 pound boneless, skinless bluegill fillets
- ½ cup butter
- ⅔ cup cornflakes
- ¼ cup grated Parmesan cheese
- ½ teaspoon basil
- ½ teaspoon oregano
- ½ teaspoon salt
- ¼ teaspoon granulated garlic

BLEU CHEESE SAUCE
- 1 cup bleu cheese, crumbled
- ¼ cup heavy cream
- 2 tablespoons orange juice

THE FLAVORS OF THE PARMESAN AND BLEU CHEESES COMPLEMENT EACH OTHER NICELY.

DIRECTIONS

In a small bowl, mix together the crumbled bleu cheese, heavy cream and orange juice. Cover and refrigerate at least 1 hour.

In a food processor, combine the cornflakes, Parmesan cheese, basil, oregano, salt and granulated garlic. Process until very fine.

Melt the butter and coat the fillets, then cover with the cornflake mixture. Arrange in a single layer on a baking sheet. Bake at 350 degrees for 25–30 minutes. Serve with the bleu cheese sauce on the side.

HAWAIIAN CATFISH CURRY

SERVES 6

INGREDIENTS

- 1½ pounds boneless, skinless catfish fillets, cut into 1½-inch pieces
- 4 tablespoons butter
- 1 medium onion, quartered and thinly sliced
- 2 cloves garlic, minced
- 1 small bag frozen baby peas, thawed
- 1 tablespoon yellow Thai curry paste, dissolved in ¼ cup hot water
- 1 cup chicken broth
- 1 tablespoon brown sugar
- 1 tablespoon peanut butter
- 1 12-ounce can coconut milk

IF YOU HEAT THE CHICKEN STOCK IN THE MICROWAVE FOR 15 SECONDS, THE BROWN SUGAR AND PEANUT BUTTER WILL BLEND IN MUCH EASIER.

DIRECTIONS

Combine the chicken broth, brown sugar and peanut butter. Mix well.

In a large wok or sauté pan, heat the butter. Add the onion and garlic and stir-fry until the onion is translucent. Add the peas, curry and chicken broth mixture. Stir in the coconut milk and catfish. Reduce heat to low, cover and simmer 12–15 minutes or until catfish is just cooked. Do not boil! Serve over steamed rice.

PERCH PARMESAN

SERVES 4-6

INGREDIENTS

- 2 pounds boneless, skinless yellow perch fillets
- 1 cup olive oil
- 3 cloves garlic, minced
- 1½ cups Parmesan cheese, finely grated
- 1½ cups cracker crumbs, finely processed
- 2 teaspoons Italian seasoning

DIRECTIONS

Mix the olive oil and garlic in a large bowl. Add the perch and marinate 20 minutes, turning several times to coat all sides.

Place cheese, cracker crumbs and Italian seasoning in a large plastic bag and shake to mix. Place several fillets in the bag at a time to coat. Transfer to a well-oiled baking pan. Bake at 350 degrees for 12–14 minutes or until the fish flakes with a fork.

IF YOU HAPPEN TO HAVE A LOT OF PERCH,
COAT THEM IN THE CHEESE MIXTURE AND
FREEZE THEM INDIVIDUALLY FOR FUTURE USE.

PACIFIC RIM WALLEYE

SERVES 4

INGREDIENTS
* 2 pounds walleye fillet, skin on

MARINADE
* ⅓ cup teriyaki sauce
* ⅓ cup port wine
* ⅓ cup orange or pineapple juice
* ¼ cup brown sugar
* ⅓ cup green onion, sliced
* 3 cloves garlic, minced
* 2 tablespoons sesame oil
* 1 tablespoon toasted sesame seeds

THIS MARINADE WORKS VERY WELL WITH PORK. A TRADITIONAL HAWAIIAN LUAU WOULD FEATURE BOTH FISH AND PORK.

DIRECTIONS
In a medium bowl, mix all marinade ingredients. Arrange the walleye fillets in a single layer in a 11"x9" baking dish. Reserving ½ cup of the marinade, pour the rest over the fillets, turning to coat. Cover with plastic warp and refrigerate for 3 hours, turning the fillets occasionally.

Prepare the grill for medium, indirect heat, and spray cooking grate with non-stick vegetable coating. Drain the walleye and discard the marinade. Arrange fillets on the cooking grate. Cover and cook 4 minutes. Baste with reserved marinade. Turn fillets and grill 4–5 minutes longer, covered. Fish should be firm, opaque and begin to flake. Baste occasionally during the final minutes of grilling.

BAKED TROUT WITH HERBED BREAD STUFFING

SERVES 4

INGREDIENTS

- 4 whole stream-variety trout, dressed
- 1 package bread stuffing mix
- ⅛ teaspoon thyme
- ⅛ teaspoon sage
- 4 tablespoons green onion, minced
- 4 tablespoons melted butter
- 4 romaine lettuce leaves, blanched

FOR A MOISTER AND MORE DENSE STUFFING, ADD BEATEN EGG TO THE STUFFING MIXTURE.

DIRECTIONS

Rinse the trout thoroughly under cold running water, pat dry and refrigerate.

Prepare the dressing according to package directions, adding the thyme, sage and green onion. Divide the stuffing into 4 portions and fill each trout cavity. Wrap a blanched romaine leaf around each trout to hold in the stuffing. Place each trout on a buttered square of heavy-duty aluminum foil. Brush the top with butter and seal the edges of the foil.

Place foil packets on a rack in a shallow pan and bake for 40 minutes.

SALMON EN CROUTE

SERVES 4

INGREDIENTS

- 4 6-ounce pieces salmon fillets
- 3 slices bacon, cut into p-inch dice
- 1 tablespoon sweet butter
- 3 tablespoons onion, diced
- 1 clove garlic, minced
- 2 tablespoons asiago cheese, shredded
- 2 cups steamed spinach, all water removed
- 1 ounce Pernod or pastis
- 9 5"x5" puff pastry sheets
- 1 egg, beaten

SERVE SALMON EN CROUTE WITH HOLLANDAISE SAUCE AND DELIGHT YOUR GUESTS AS THEY SAVOR THE STEAMY LICORICE FLAVOR OF THIS DISH.

DIRECTIONS

Sauté the bacon, onion and garlic in the butter, until bacon is slightly rendered and the onion is translucent. Remove pan from the heat and stir in the cheese, spinach and Pernod. Season to taste with salt and pepper. Chill mixture at least 1 hour before proceeding.

Place salmon fillets, skin side down, on work surface. Place ¼ cup of the spinach mixture on each fillet and roll into a cylinder. Chill at least 1 hour before proceeding.

Roll out 2 pieces of puff pastry large enough to cover a salmon roll overlapping by 1½ inches on each side. Place salmon on 1 piece of the pastry and brush edges of pastry with beaten egg. Drape the 2nd piece of pastry over the salmon. Trim edges and seal by roll folding the edges. Repeat these steps for the remaining salmon rolls.

Cut decorative shapes from the remaining pastry piece. Brush top of pastry with beaten egg and place cutout on top of each salmon en croute. Bake at 400 degrees for 20 minutes or until golden brown.

BAKED BLUEGILL FILLETS WITH CRISPY WISCONSIN CHEESE

SERVES 6

INGREDIENTS

* 2 pounds boneless, skinless bluegill fillets
* ¼ teaspoon salt
* ⅛ teaspoon white pepper
* 3 cups whole wheat bread, cut into ½-inch cubes
* 8 tablespoons butter
* 1 medium onion, minced
* 1 tablespoon dijon mustard
* 1½ cups grated Wisconsin cheddar cheese
* ⅓ cup chopped parsley

DIRECTIONS

Season fillets with salt and pepper and place in a buttered baking dish. Lightly toast the bread cubes. In a large non-stick skillet, melt the butter. Add the onion and reduce the heat to low. Cover and cook until translucent, 5–6 minutes. Stir in the mustard and mix in the bread cubes. Add the cheese and parsley, mixing well.

Spread the cheese mixture over the fillets. Bake in a 325 degree oven for 25–30 minutes or until fish flakes with a fork.

FOR SOMETHING SPECIAL, SUBSTITUTE
BLEU CHEESE FOR THE CHEDDAR.

SPICY CRAYFISH AND CHICKEN

SERVES 4-6

INGREDIENTS

- ¾ pound crayfish tails, shelled
- 1½ pounds boneless, skinless chicken breasts, cut into ½-inch dice
- 4 tablespoons butter
- 1½ teaspoons chopped garlic
- 6 slices thick bacon, cut into ½-inch dice
- 1 teaspoon Italian seasoning
- 2 cups medium-spicy salsa

WHITE SAUCE

- 2 tablespoons butter
- 1 tablespoon flour
- 1 cup chicken or fish stock
- 1 cup heavy cream
- ⅛ teaspoon nutmeg
- salt and pepper
- 2 cups medium-spicy salsa

IF YOU CANNOT TOLERATE THE SPICE IN THE SALSA, USE CHOPPED STEWED TOMATOES INSTEAD.

DIRECTIONS

To prepare the white sauce, melt the butter in a saucepan. Whisk in the flour. Slowly whisk in the cream and stock. Whisk over low heat until thickened. Add the nutmeg and season to taste with salt and pepper. Stir in the salsa.

In a heavy 4-quart dutch oven, melt the butter and sauté the bacon over medium heat. Stir in the garlic and add the chicken and crayfish. Cover and reduce the heat to low. Simmer for 10–15 minutes, stirring occasionally. Add the white sauce to this mixture. Simmer over low heat for 15 minutes or until thoroughly heated. If the sauce is too thick, stir in additional cream.

Serve over noodles or steamed rice.

BAKED SUCKER CASSEROLE

SERVES 4-6

INGREDIENTS

- 3 cups boneless, skinless steamed sucker
  (approximately 2 pounds), cut into bite-size pieces
- ½ cup chopped onion
- ½ cup chopped celery
- ¼ cup butter
- 3 tablespoons flour
- 2 cups milk or cream
- 1 can peas and carrots, drained
- salt and pepper to taste

DIRECTIONS

Melt the butter and sauté the onion and celery for 3–4 minutes or until slightly browned. Reduce the heat and stir in the flour. Gradually whisk in the milk, stirring until thickened. Season to taste with salt and pepper. Stir in the peas and carrots and add the fish.

Place mixture in a buttered loaf pan and bake at 325 degrees for 20–30 minutes. Serve over buttered noodles or toast points.

PRIOR TO STEAMING THE FISH, REMOVE ANY FAT
FROM THE BELLY AND DORSAL FIN AREA OF THE
FILLET. STEAMING ALLOWS FOR EASY REMOVAL
OF THE SKIN AND ANY REMAINING BONES.

GREEK STYLE PAN FISH

SERVES 4-6

INGREDIENTS
- 2 pounds boneless pan fish fillets
- Cavender's All Purpose Greek Seasoning
- 2 sweet red peppers, seeded and cut into ¼-inch strips
- 2 green bell peppers, seeded and cut into ¼-inch strips
- 1 large onion, peeled, sliced and cut in half
- 1 15-ounce can stewed tomatoes, chopped
- 1 stick butter

DIRECTIONS
Preheat oven to 325 degrees. Butter a 9"x12" baking dish.

In a large sauté pan, melt the butter, add the peppers and onion and stir-fry over medium heat until cooked but still crisp. Stir in the stewed tomatoes and cook for 3 minutes. Set aside.

Liberally season the fish with Cavender's and arrange in the baking dish. Top with the cooked vegetables and stewed tomatoes. Bake for 1 hour.

TO MAKE THIS DISH A LITTLE MORE FESTIVE, TOP
WITH ZUCCHINI, BLACK OLIVES AND FETA CHEESE.

BASS CAKES WITH SPICY TARTER SAUCE

SERVES 4

INGREDIENTS

- 1 pound boneless, skinless bass fillets, finely chopped
- ¾ pound peeled and boiled potatoes, shredded
- 2 tablespoons butter
- 1 medium onion, peeled, sliced and chopped
- 1 tablespoon fresh cilantro, chopped
- 1 teaspoon lemon juice
- 1 large egg, beaten
- flour mixed with fine cracker meal
- ⅓ cup vegetable oil

THESE CAKES MAKE A GREAT SANDWICH. ADD LETTUCE AND TOMATO FOR A NORTHWOODS BLT.

TARTER SAUCE

- 2 cups mayonnaise
- 2 tablespoons coarse mustard
- 1 tablespoon worcestershire sauce
- few drops green Tabasco
- 1 teaspoon sugar

DIRECTIONS

In a medium bowl, mix together all tarter sauce ingredients. Cover and refrigerate.

In a large bowl, combine the bass, cilantro and lemon juice. Mix the egg with the shredded potatoes and gently fold into the bass mixture. Divide this mixture into 8 portions and shape into ½-inch thick cakes. Dredge the cakes in the flour and cracker meal mixture.

Heat the vegetable oil in a large sauté pan. Add the bass cakes and fry for 3–4 minutes on each side or until crisp and golden. Drain on paper towel and serve with the tarter sauce.

TEMPURA CATFISH

SERVES 4

INGREDIENTS
- 8 catfish fillets
- 1 cup flour
- frying oil, heated to 375 degrees

TEMPURA BATTER
- 1½ cups flour
- 1 teaspoon salt
- 1 tablespoon canola oil
- 2 egg yolks, beaten
- ¾ cups beer

THIS SHOULD BE YOUR GO-TO BATTER FOR VEGETABLES, MEAT AND FISH.

DIRECTIONS
In a large bowl, mix together the flour, salt, oil and eggs. Gradually add the beer. Cover and refrigerate 3–4 hours.

Dust the fillets with flour, then dip in batter just before frying, shaking off any excess. Fry fillets until they are light brown and they float. Keep fillets warm in a 200 degree oven until ready to serve.

WHITEFISH WITH VEGETABLES

SERVES 4-6

INGREDIENTS

- 1 pound whitefish fillets, cut into serving pieces
- 1 small cabbage, cored and sliced
- 1 15-ounce can stewed tomatoes
- 1 large carrot, peeled and thinly sliced
- 2 chicken bouillon cubes, dissolved in 2 cups hot water

DIRECTIONS

In a large saucepan, simmer cabbage, tomatoes, carrot and bouillon for 20 minutes or until the cabbage is tender. Lay whitefish over the vegetables and simmer 10–12 minutes or until fish flakes.

ADD HEAVY CREAM TO THE COOKING LIQUID TO MAKE A MUCH RICHER SAUCE. SEASON WITH SALT AND PEPPER TO TASTE.

ENGLISH STYLE FISH AND CHIPS

SERVES 6

INGREDIENTS

- 2 pounds boneless, skinless fish fillets, your choice
- 2 cups self-rising flour
- ⅔ cup cold water
- ⅓ cup beer

- 1½ pounds potatoes, peeled
- oil for deep frying
- lemon wedges
- malt vinegar

THE BATTER IN THIS RECIPE IS VERY SIMILAR TO A TEMPURA BATTER AND CAN BE USED WITH SHRIMP OR VEGETABLES, AS WELL AS THE FISH FILLETS.

DIRECTIONS

In a large bowl, mix a pinch of salt with the flour. Gradually whisk in the water and beer to make a smooth batter. Cover and set aside for at least 30 minutes.

Cut the potatoes lengthwise into slices m-inch thick, then into m-inch wide strips. Rinse under cold running water. Drain and dry well.

Heat the oil in a deep fryer or heavy fry pan to 300 degrees. Using a wire basket, fry the potatoes in small batches for 5–6 minutes or until soft but not brown. Remove from oil and drain on paper towels.

Increase the oil temperature to 375 degrees. Stir the batter and coat the fish fillets, placing on a rack to drain excess batter.

Working in batches and using a basket, deep fry the fish for 6–8 minutes until the fish floats and is golden brown. Drain on paper towels and keep warm.

Again, working in batches, return the potatoes to the oil and fry for 2–3 minutes until golden brown and crisp. Drain and keep hot. Sprinkle with salt. Serve with malt vinegar and lemon wedges.

PIKE WITH BACON IN CREAM SAUCE

SERVES 4-6

INGREDIENTS

- 2 pounds boneless, skinless pike fillets
- 8 slices bacon, cooked and chopped
- 1 cup white wine
- 1 cup water
- 1 teaspoon salt
- 1 tablespoon lemon juice
- 1 can condensed cream of celery soup
- 2 cups heavy cream
- 1 cup mild salsa

DIRECTIONS

Place fish in a large saucepan with water, salt and wine. Bring to a boil, reduce heat to low, cover and simmer for 10–12 minutes or until the fish flakes with a fork. Remove the fish from the liquid, cool and break into bite-size pieces.

In a 2-quart pot, combine the soup and cream. Heat over low heat, stirring constantly, until bubbly. Stir in the bacon and salsa and fold in the fish. Heat until hot. Spoon over steamed rice or wide noodles.

REDUCE THE AMOUNT OF CREAM TO
1 CUP AND USE THIS AS A PARTY DIP
WITH NACHOS OR TACO CHIPS.

BACON BASTED PERCH

SERVES 1

INGREDIENTS

- Dressed perch, 1 large or 2 small per serving, heads on or off (your choice)
- 2 strips bacon for large perch, or 1 strip bacon for small perch
- stemmed fresh parsley
- salt and pepper
- fresh lemon juice

DIRECTIONS

Moisten the outside of the perch with a few drops of lemon juice and season the inside with salt and pepper. Stuff the body cavity with parsley. Wrap bacon diagonally around the fish with the end on the bottom side.

Place the fish on a baking sheet that has been treated with a vegetable spray.

Bake for 20–25 minutes in a 325 degree oven or until the internal temperature reaches 165 degrees and the bacon is crisp. Garnish individual servings with chopped parsley and lemon wedges or slices.

TRY THIS TECHNIQUE WITH OTHER SMALL-
BODIED FISH LIKE TROUT. YOU WILL
ENJOY THE SAVORY, SMOKEY TASTE.

WALLEYE IN TOMATO SAUCE

SERVES 6

INGREDIENTS

- 1 pound boneless, skinless walleye fillets, cut into 1-inch pieces
- 2 tablespoons vegetable oil
- 1 tablespoon olive oil
- 1 teaspoon garlic, chopped
- 1 small onion, chopped
- 2 15-ounce cans stewed tomatoes, chopped
- 2 8-ounce cans tomato sauce
- ½ cup dry white wine
- salt to taste
- 1 teaspoon brown sugar
- ½ teaspoon dried oregano
- ½ teaspoon dried basil
- grated Parmesan cheese

DIRECTIONS

In a large heavy pot, heat the oils. Add the garlic and onion, and sauté lightly. Add the tomatoes, tomato sauce and wine. Bring to a boil. Reduce the heat to low and simmer, stirring frequently for 20 minutes, adding water as necessary. Add salt, brown sugar, oregano and basil. Adjust seasoning to taste. Add the walleye and continue simmering 3–5 minutes or until the fish is fully cooked. Serve with hot pasta and grated Parmesan cheese.

TO GIVE YOUR SAUCE ADDED BODY,

INCLUDE 1 SMALL CAN OF MINCED CLAMS.

SMOKED SALMON AND GREEN ONION IN CREAM SAUCE

SERVES 4

INGREDIENTS
- 1 pound smoked salmon
- 3 tablespoons green onion, minced
- 1 15-ounce can stewed tomatoes, drained and chopped

WHITE SAUCE
- 2 tablespoons sweet butter
- 2 tablespoons flour
- 1 cup chicken, veal or fish stock
- 1 cup heavy cream
- nutmeg
- salt and pepper

SIMPLE BUT SO VERY ELEGANT.

DIRECTIONS
In a stainless steel saucepan, melt the butter over low heat. Whisk in flour and slowly add the stock and cream, stirring until well blended. Stirring constantly, heat the sauce until thickened. Add a pinch of nutmeg and salt and pepper to taste.

Julienne slice the salmon across the grain. Add the salmon, green onion and tomatoes to the heated white sauce and simmer 10 minutes. Serve over fresh pasta or steamed rice.

TUSCAN BASS FILLETS

SERVES 6

INGREDIENTS

- 2 pounds boneless, skinless bass fillets
- 4 tablespoons olive oil
- 1 medium onion, finely chopped
- ½ cup celery, thinly sliced
- 1 15-ounce can stewed tomatoes, chopped
- 1 cup tomato vegetable juice
- ½ cup salad olives, sliced
- ⅛ teaspoon white pepper
- 2 cloves garlic, minced (optional)
- 1 teaspoon brown sugar

DIRECTIONS

Arrange bass fillets in a well-oiled shallow baking dish.

Heat the olive oil in a large non-stick skillet. Add the onion and celery and cook until the onion is tender and the celery is slightly crunchy. Stir in the tomatoes, juice, olives, pepper, garlic and brown sugar.

Bake in a 325 degree oven for 30–40 minutes or until the fish flakes. Serve over pasta.

IF YOU DON'T CARE FOR OLIVES,
TRY ADDING ANCHOVY PASTE—
A HEALTHY SALT SUBSTITUTE.

ONE-POT CISCO MEAL

SERVES 2-4

INGREDIENTS
* 2 15-ounce cans stewed tomatoes
* 1 pound boneless, skinless cisco fillets
* 2 cups cooked rice, mixed with 2 cups tomato juice
* salt and pepper

DIRECTIONS
Place stewed tomatoes in a heavy sauté pan and bring to a boil. Reduce heat to medium and season to taste with salt and pepper. Lay the cisco fillets on top of the tomatoes, spread the rice over the fish and cover. Cook over medium heat until the tomatoes start to simmer, 5–8 minutes. Reduce heat to medium-low, cover and cook for 15–20 minutes without removing the lid.

Serve when fish flakes and the rice is hot.

ADD COOKED VEGETABLES, SUCH
AS CORN OR PEAS, TO THE RICE
TO ROUND OUT THIS DISH.

GRILLED SALMON

INGREDIENTS

- 2 pounds boneless salmon fillets, trimmed of all fat
- teriyaki sauce
- brown sugar
- 1 large onion, sliced
- olive oil
- heavy duty aluminum foil

DIRECTIONS

Cut a piece of foil large enough to wrap a salmon fillet. Brush the skin side with olive oil. Place a layer of onion on the foil and top with a salmon fillet. Baste with teriyaki and sprinkle with brown sugar. Seal the foil and place on a medium-hot grill. Cook for 30–40 minutes or until the salmon flakes.

THIS SALMON WILL BE SWEET AND SAVORY.
CHECK FOR DONENESS AT 35 MINUTES. OPEN
THE FOIL CAREFULLY TO AVOID STEAM BURNS.

CRAYFISH QUICHE

SERVES 4-6

PASTRY
- ¼ pound butter
- 1⅓ cup flour
- ¼ cup cold water

FILLING
- 4 tablespoons bacon, cooked and crumbled
- 2 cups crayfish tails, cooked, shelled and coarsely chopped
- 2 tablespoons green onion, chopped
- ½ cup grated swiss cheese
- 4 large eggs
- 2 cups heavy cream
- ⅛ teaspoon salt
- ⅛ teaspoon white pepper
- ⅛ teaspoon nutmeg

TO CHANGE THE FLAVOR PROFILE, SUBSTITUTE CHORIZO SAUSAGE FOR THE BACON.

DIRECTIONS
Prepare the pastry crust by placing the flour in a food processor fitted with a stainless blade. Cut the butter into small pieces. Add to the flour and pulse chop until grainy. Turn the food processor on and gradually add the cold water. Process until a ball of dough forms. Roll the dough out and place in a 10-inch pie tin.

Distribute the bacon, crayfish, green onion and cheese over the bottom of the pastry shell.

Whisk together the eggs, cream, salt, pepper and nutmeg. Pour over the crayfish mixture in the pastry shell. Bake in a 325 degree oven for 35–40 minutes or until the top is golden brown and the custard is set. Let the quiche cool slightly before serving.

APPLE FESTIVAL LAKE TROUT

INGREDIENTS

- 2 pounds boneless, skinless lake trout fillets
- 2 medium onions, thinly sliced
- 3 medium apples, peeled, cored and sliced
- 1½ cups apple cider
- 1 bay leaf
- 1 small lemon, thinly sliced

SPICE MIX

- 1 teaspoon celery salt
- ½ teaspoon white pepper
- ⅛ teaspoon crushed oregano

DIRECTIONS

Sprinkle spice mix sparingly over the fillets and place in a buttered baking dish. Layer the apples and onions over the fish, topped with the lemon slices. Pour cider over the trout. Add the bay leaf, cover with foil and bake at 325 degrees for 20–30 minutes or until the fish flakes.

STEP UP THE FLAVORS BY SUBSTITUTING 3/4 CUP
RIESLING WINE FOR HALF OF THE APPLE CIDER.

OVEN POACHED LAKE PERCH

SERVES 6

PASTRY
- 2 pounds lake perch fillets
- 1 cup carrots, julienne-sliced
- 1 cup celery, julienne-sliced
- 1 cup sweet onion, thinly sliced
- 1 tablespoon dried cranberries, chopped
- 2 tablespoons green olives, chopped
- 1 teaspoon fresh basil, chopped
- 2 cups clam juice
- 1 cup heavy cream
- 2 tablespoons sweet butter

POACHING LENDS
AN ELEGANT TWIST
TO THE USUALLY
PAN-FRIED PERCH.

DIRECTIONS
Butter a large baking dish. Mix together the carrot, celery, onion, dried cranberries and olives and distribute evenly in the bottom of the baking dish. Sprinkle with the basil.

Fold perch fillets in half, skin side in, and place in the baking dish, overlapping slightly. Add clam juice and cover the fish with buttered parchment paper.

Bake in a 350 degree oven for 15–20 minutes. Strain cooking liquid into a saucepan and return the fish to the oven to keep warm.

Over medium heat, reduce liquid by one-half. Add the cream and gradually whisk in butter. Adjust seasoning with salt and pepper to taste. Just before serving, sauce the fish.

FETTUCCINE WITH SMOKED SALMON IN BUTTER SAUCE

SERVES 4

INGREDIENTS

- 6 ounces smoked salmon, thinly sliced and cut into strips
- 2 medium zucchini squash
- 1 stick of butter, softened
- 1½ cups heavy cream
- zest from 1 orange
- 2 tablespoons orange juice
- 1 tablespoon fresh dill, chopped
- ½ tablespoon fresh basil, finely chopped
- 8 ounces dry fettuccine, cooked according to package directions
- salt and pepper to taste

DIRECTIONS

Cut the squash in half lengthwise and use a spoon to remove the seeds. Thinly slice the zucchini halves.

In a large sauté pan, melt the butter. Add the zucchini, orange zest, orange juice, dill and basil. Reduce the heat to low and cook 2–3 minutes, stirring occasionally. Add the cream and season with salt and pepper. Stir in the salmon and add reheated pasta. Cook for 2–3 minutes. Transfer to a heated serving bowl or platter. Serve with freshly grated cheese.

ADD CARROT COINS TO THIS DISH FOR ADDITIONAL FLAVOR, TEXTURE AND COLOR. PRECOOK THE CARROTS AND ADD THEM WITH THE SALMON.

INDEX